...ON THE OPEN UNIVERSITY, MILTON KEYNES

...ive essays
...es in sociology
...Sociologists', this series

qu...

How di...

How might ...nature
rights better serve the glob...

In so doing, Woodiwiss explains ...
in the distinctive ways it did in fou...
Japan and the UN. On this basis he p...
sociological account of the developmen...
discourse. This account represents a strikin...
and policy in this increasingly fraught but...
global concern.

Anthony Woodiwiss is Dean of Social Sciences ...
London. He is the author of numerous articles and books ...
Human Rights Work Globally and *Globalization, Human Rig...
Law in Pacific Asia.

SERIES EDITOR: PETER HAMILTON

Designed to compliment the successful [...]
covers the main concepts, issues, debates and contro[...]
and the social sciences. The series aims to provide authorita[...]
on central topics of social science, such as community, power, w[...]
sexuality, inequality, benefits and ideology, class and family. Books adopt
a strong 'individual' line, as critical essays rather than literature surveys,
offering lively and original treatments of their subject matter. The books
will be useful to students and teachers of sociology, political science,
economics, psychology, philosophy and geography.

Citizenship
KEITH FAULKS

Class
STEPHEN EDGELL

Community
GERARD DELANTY

Consumption
ROBERT BOCOCK

Culture
CHRIS JENKS

Globalization – second edition
MALCOLM WATERS

Lifestyle
DAVID CHANEY

Mass Media
PIERRE SORLIN

Moral Panics
KENNETH THOMPSON

Old Age
JOHN VINCENT

Postmodernity
BARRY SMART

Racism – second edition
ROBERT MILES AND
MALCOLM BROWN

Risk
DEBORAH LUPTON

Sexuality – second edition
JEFFREY WEEKS

Social Capital
JOHN FIELD

Transgression
CHRIS JENKS

The Virtual
ROB SHIELDS

Social Identity – second edition
RICHARD JENKINS

Culture – second edition
CHRIS JENKS

Human Rights
ANTHONY WOODIWISS

HUMAN RIGHTS

Anthony Woodiwiss

Routledge
Taylor & Francis Group

LONDON AND NEW YORK

First published 2005
by Routledge
2 Park Square, Milton Park, Abingdon, Oxon OX14 4RN

Simultaneously published in the USA and Canada
by Routledge
270 Madison Ave, New York, NY 10016

Routledge is an imprint of the Taylor & Francis Group

Typeset in Garamond and Scala by
Keystroke, Jacaranda Lodge, Wolverhampton
Printed and bound in Great Britain by
TJ International Ltd, Padstow, Cornwall

British Library Cataloguing in Publication Data
A catalogue record for this book is available from the British Library

Library of Congress Cataloging in Publication Data
A catalog record for this book has been requested

ISBN 0–415–36069–2 (pbk)
ISBN 0–415–36068–4 (hbk)

For Hideo and Chizuko

We're sometimes faulted for a naive faith that liberty can change the world. If that's an error, it began with reading too much John Locke and Adam Smith.

(George W. Bush, London, 19 November 2003)

The history of the freedoms accorded to man has, unto this day, been repeatedly confused with the history of the freedoms accorded by man to the economy.

(Raoul Vaneigem, 2003)

We do not understand political reality well enough to be pessimistic, or for that matter, optimistic.

(Richard Falk, 2000)

CONTENTS

Acknowledgements

As I sat down to write these acknowledgements, I was struck by the cheering realisation that I had been working in the area of the sociology of rights for thirty years. Cheering because I realised that it had been such interesting work that it seemed like only yesterday that I had spent a summer or two (those were the days!) working on my first very long and very rough paper on the development of American labour law in the kitchen of my dear friend Terry Wordingham's flat in Maida Vale – still the largest and most comfortable of all of the many kitchens in which I have written. Cheering also, if somewhat more ambivalently, because, as the reader will quickly discover, there is still so much to be done, so much to be corrected and improved upon.

In my earlier work I was concerned to develop the theory necessary to make sense of the rights/society relation by engaging in a number of national case studies (Woodiwiss, 1990a, 1990b, 1992). In my last book I completed a shift of focus from the national to the global level that had begun in *Globalisation, Human Rights and Labour Law in Pacific Asia* (1998). Thus *Making Human Rights Work Globally* (2003) draws some analytical and practical lessons from my case studies for understanding and enhancing the human rights of labour at the global level. In the present text, my concern is to synthesise and develop what I have learnt so far about human rights in general.

Globally focused though the present book may be, and in the case of human rights at least, the local is both the source of the global and where the global is lived by most of us. The methodological significance of this is that the comparative method continues to be a valid mode of sociological reasoning – indeed so much so that in my view the value of much currently available work on globalisation is vitiated by its authors' lack of knowledge of any societies other than their own. For this reason, I have developed a good part of the argument that follows by discussing, relating and comparing or contrasting developments in three of the societies – England, the United States and Japan – that were amongst my earliest case studies: England because that is where contemporary rights discourse originated; the United States because it was the most influential state in the formation of our current human rights regime; and Japan because it stands as the classic example of what happens to rights discourse when it is successfully embedded in a non-western society, as we heard so many times in the months preceding the recent occupation of Iraq. Thus the accounts of legal developments in these societies are derived from my earlier work. However, these accounts have been shortened and simplified to improve their readability as well as checked for accuracy and, more often, plausibility against more recent scholarship. These accounts have also been significantly developed in various ways so that they may contribute to the new analysis of the nature and development of human rights presented here. Nevertheless, and despite the fact that most of the source texts are also out of print, I still feel it necessary to acknowledge and thank Pluto Press (Woodiwiss, 1990a), Berg (Woodiwiss, 1990b), and Routledge (Woodiwiss, 1992) for their permissions to use material previously published by them.

Finally, I would like to thank the following for various forms of essential advice, help and support: Aya Tokita, Frank Pearce, Costas Douzinas, Bandit, Rod Broadhurst, Maxine Molyneux, Fehti Acikel, Bryan Turner, Stephen Chiu, Howard Tumber, John Solomos, Alice Bloch, Mireille Hebing, Kerry Lee and all my other excellent students, colleagues, academic and non-academic, in the Department of Sociology at City.

Clerkenwell, July 2004

Introduction

Rights and power

Put as plainly as possible, but to take sides immediately, the term 'rights' refers to a legally enforceable set of expectations as to how others, most obviously the state, should behave towards rights bearers. These expectations may take the form of limitations on, and/or requirements of, the behaviour of others. Rights bearers have to be entities legally considered to possess 'personality' – that is, legally deemed to be autonomous moral agents – and therefore capable of taking decisions and accepting responsibilities, as in the case of adult persons, trade unions, corporations, or states. More controversially, rights bearers may also be members of groups legally recognised as entitled to make claims to protection and/or support on the basis of the principle of reciprocity[1] because they have been denied the possibility of autonomy as a result of factors such as age (children), race, gender, sexual orientation, poverty, mental or physical illness, or indigeneousness. With respect to individuals, the initial bearers of rights, the limitations or requirements placed on others may relate to the bearer's person, property or other individualised and legally specified relationships or expectations.

When I say that with such an understanding I will 'take sides immediately', the debate I have in mind is that between the supporters of natural law theory and the Legal Positivists concerning the nature of rights (for an excellent introduction to this debate, see Jones, 1994). According to natural law theory, certain rights exist independently of, or prior to, the law and are therefore intrinsic to human beings, whether as individuals or members of groups, in the sense that humans are born with them. For the Legal Positivists, by contrast, all rights are extrinsic to individuals and groups in that they are created and attached to legal persons by external forces, notably by legislative acts or judicial decisions. So distinguished, it should be immediately clear why a sociologist would side with the Legal Positivist camp: to put it slightly flippantly, Legal Positivism leaves space for sociological input as regards understanding the development of rights and their attachment to their bearers, whilst natural law theory prefers to fill that space with divinations of one kind or another.

According to majority, educated western opinion, the natural law theorist John Locke was most likely correct, or at least wise, when he argued that some at least of the set of ideas we now know as human rights had their origins in what he understood as the god-given, universal state of freedom that preceded the drawing up of the social contract:

> Men being, as has been said, by nature all free, equal, and independent, no one can be put out of this estate and subjected to the political power of another without his own consent, which is done by agreeing with other men, to join and unite into a community for their comfortable, safe, and peaceable living, one amongst another, in a secure enjoyment of their properties, and a greater security against any that are not of it. This any number of men may do, because it injures not the freedom of the rest; they are left, as they were, in the liberty of the state of Nature. When any number of men have so consented to make one community or government, they are thereby presently incorporated, and make one body politic, wherein the majority have a right to act and conclude the rest.
>
> (Locke, 1689, para. 95)

The same body of opinion consequently regards human rights as the inalienable property of all individuals throughout the world, as theirs simply because they are human. Unsurprisingly, then, the prominence currently given to human rights by our governments and media is regarded by many of us in the West as providing confirmation of our civilised condition. Not only do we assume that our own social arrangements are premised historically and presently on respect for such rights, but we also evince great interest in, and considerable concern for, the human rights of others presumed to be less fortunate than ourselves. We are therefore generally happy that our governments and especially our NGOs appear to be ceaselessly campaigning for this good cause both at home and in faraway places.

By contrast, Jeremy Bentham, one of the founders of Legal Positivism, once famously declared natural rights to be 'nonsense upon stilts'. Much of what follows depends upon a sociological line of argument that has generally been used to justify Bentham-like dismissals of the meaningfulness of rights talk. Here, however, this argument will be used to provide the basis for a defence of human rights. What follows may therefore be described as a sceptic's defence of human rights.

Fittingly, then, I will begin with a sceptical question: 'If human rights are rooted in our common humanity, why do they remain controversial, especially amongst intellectuals on the left and in many parts of the developing world?'[2] The most obvious current answer would be to point to what many consider to be the unfortunate association between human rights and the 'coalition of the willing' that presently occupies Iraq – a coalition unilaterally willing to deploy massive military force and therefore to intentionally sacrifice uncounted (literally) thousands of innocent lives in the defence of the human rights of those same innocents because they live in an ill-governed but highly selective set of states.[3] Combining advocacy of the idea of the privileged character of human freedom with the slaughter, torture and humiliation of innocents produces a sharp dissonance in most minds and not just in those of professionally sensitive intellectuals. Moreover, such dissonance, if not such violence, has characterised what has become known as the 'human rights project' ever since its inception in 1948 when the General Assembly of the United Nations adopted the Universal Declaration of Human Rights (UDHR). On that occasion several states, notably the Soviet Union, abstained from voting for the UDHR because they felt that the idea of a common humanity had been hijacked by adherents to a particular ideology, namely 'bourgeois individualism'. Since that time, non-white peoples, women, sexual minorities, developing countries, and non-western cultures more generally have also discovered or felt that they had been excluded from the UDHR's conception of a common humanity. In all such cases the excluded parties have resorted to political action in an effort to reverse their exclusion. Sometimes they have been successful. More often they have not, and their complaints of exclusion have typically been dismissed as groundless, at least initially. However, most of the aggrieved parties have responded by insisting that such dismissals simply compound the neglect of the rights violations of which they complain. How, then, is it possible that human rights can be invoked both to deny and to criticise such exclusions? How can human rights provide the bases for both the exercise of power and its critique?

As a consequence of the history of repeated dissonances and political conflict, it has gradually become clear that issues such as what should count as a human right, the universality or otherwise of the present array of rights, and indeed the very idea of a common humanity, are not simply matters of intellectual controversy but also matters of power, not simply matters of philosophy and law but also matters of social structure and politics. Thus the deeper reason why the controversial character of human rights is not so much 'unfortunate' as inevitable is that any rights regime, whether international or national, may now be seen as an index representing the disposition of power in the pertinent jurisdiction. Consequently, when read sociologically, the coverage, content, inclusions, and exclusions of rights texts tell us not only who is protected against what, but also the sort of people and the aspects of social relations that are especially valued (or not) by the governmental body responsible for constructing, approving and enforcing the regime.

Accurate though I believe this alternative understanding of the nature of rights regimes to be, and the main body of the present text is constructed on the basis that it is accurate, it is a development that carries certain dangers. Especially dangerous, I think, is the suggestion one hears increasingly often from those angered by the numerous hypocrisies that have been and remain part of human rights thought and practice, namely that a politics grounded in an optimistic view of human nature would be better able to protect individuals than the law since the latter is grounded in a pessimistic view that almost invites victimisation (Badiou, 2001). To my mind, this is very unlikely to be the case. Although it is true that sometimes in the past such a politics has provided an effective means of ending such hypocrisies, it has also been the cause of many of the denied or neglected abuses that gave rise to the charges of hypocrisy in the first place. This is because optimistic political projects have tended to reject any ethical constraints with the result that, as history attests, the pursuit of the good has all too easily been transformed into the administration of evil. The law may indeed be where various hypocrisies are most deeply embedded, hence what I refer to below as the 'paradox of human rights'. However, not only did the law, in the form of 'the rule of law', gain its presently exhalted role in western social life as a means of both constraining and facilitating political and especially state actions, but in this form it is also a self-limiting activity in that it is rule-bound as well as rule-enforcing. Thus, if society's aspirations are reasonably quickly entrusted to the law, they are far less likely to produce monsters than if these aspirations remain solely objects of political calculation. Indeed, as the critics stress, the main danger in entrusting anything to the law is that nothing at all will happen.

In a country like Britain there are millions of legal events every day – ranging from street cautions, through arrests, bankruptcies, contract signings and property sales, to imprisonments – but one's sense of their significance is greatly diminished once it is remembered that billions of other social events also take place every day that are not subject to direct legal intervention. The disproportion between human rights related legal events and social events with a potential human rights content is in all probability even greater, since human rights tend not to be proactively enforced, whether by specialised agencies (as in the case of the criminal law) or through requirements to follow certain legally specified forms of action (as in the case of the civil law). Instead, human rights, where they are enforced at all, tend to be reactively enforced on the basis of victim complaints and, moreover, only in relation to a narrow range of social interactions. Human rights, then, tend to be legally enforced only at the extremities of social life. This suggests, however, not that legal regulation should be abandoned but that legal enforcement strategies should take account of two sociologically generated and related considerations. First, enforcement mainly depends on the ordinary respectfulness or oppressiveness of daily life, especially as regards relations between citizens and representatives of the state. This indicates that the most effective enforcement strategy would be a preventative but still legislatively and legally mediated one that attends to the causes of violations as well as punishes violators. Second, to be effective the legal enforcement of human rights must not only be incorporated into the criminal and civil law but also, and most importantly, it must mobilise the supportive elements and/or processes present within the social routines of everyday life. In sum, it is the impossibility of the law's omnipresence plus the self-restraint intrinsic to it that means both that the law is socially safe, or at least safer than politics, and that human rights interventions must be sociologically and locally informed as well as both preventative and reactive, if they are to have any significant effect. Unfortunately, the present global human rights regime has not been constructed on this basis which it is why it is so far from being fully effective.

Thus, in line with what one might expect of what I am happy to regard as the 'science of the obvious', the broadest sociological insight with respect to human rights is that the overall structure and general tenor of social relations, the law and politics may each play important but different roles in securing and enhancing respect for human rights: the overall structure and tenor of social relations determines and enforces basic expectations as regards what is acceptable or unacceptable behaviour; the law provides a potentially powerful and relatively safe means of reinforcing such expectations, since it can mobilise and focus the power of the state in a controllable way where there are particular difficulties; and politics furnishes the most important direct means of effecting change in both social expectations and reinforcement strategies. This said, these different spheres of social life are not in any sense hermetically sealed entities. Rather, they are more like 'Chinese boxes' or M.C. Escher's perspectives in that they exist inside one another. Thus they are inter-connected in many and complex ways which means that outcomes are sometimes as unexpected and unwanted as they are unintended. In the main text, I will suggest that historically the mode of interconnection has been a largely unwilled and apparently spontaneous process mediated through ideological discourses. A future task for a sociology of human rights would therefore be not simply to continue the archaeological work concerned with these processes that is reported here, but also to produce an understanding of them detailed enough to make these processes more amenable to conscious manipulation on behalf of the enhancement of human rights protections. Thus, although much of what follows will be sceptical in tone, my purpose is not to trash human rights but to contribute to their reconstruction.

AN OUTLINE OF THE ARGUMENT

What is to be presented here is a severely abridged report on work-in-progress that provides a preliminary introduction to a general sociology of human rights.[4] Part I outlines the rise, diversity and limitations of rights discourse, and consists of six chapters. Chapter 1 proposes that, and explains why, the metaphorical figure which summarises and shapes the way we think about rights should be changed from that of a 'social contract', which connotes a freely made and entirely benign agreement, to that of human sacrifice, which connotes a double-edged discourse that threatens human sacredness at the same time as it confirms it. Chapter 2 provides an account of the classical and more recent sociological literature most directly pertinent to the understanding of rights. Chapter 3 outlines the intellectual and practical development, as well as the social embedding, of the idea of a legal right from Ancient Rome to the beginning of the nineteenth century, focusing on the English and American cases. Particular attention is paid to specifying what exactly a right is and how certain rights were singled out as 'liberties' and ascribed a special status as natural rights. Chapter 4 returns briefly to the sociological literature, especially the work of Barrington Moore, in order to provide a broader and comparative social-structural context for the further examination of the case studies that follow. Chapter 5 continues the story of rights discourse in the United States and England, paying particular attention to the displacement of the value of reciprocity by that of individual autonomy and the latter's enforcement through the mode of governance known as the 'rule of law'. Chapter 6 outlines Japanese developments from the Meiji Restoration of 1868 up to the beginning of the Second World War. Significantly, in none of these cases did the benefits of the enforcement of rights discourse extend to the propertyless, who instead became subject to a 'rule of law' premised on property and/or patriarchal right.

In the course of a further five chapters, Part II outlines and discusses the development of contemporary human rights discourse and the rediscovery and reanimation of the value of reciprocity in the context of both continuing social and rights regime differences, and the ongoing process of globalisation. Chapter 7 outlines the revival of rights discourse in the early twentieth century United States and explains how this made it possible for President Roosevelt to invent the discourse of human rights in 1941 as he sought, first, to prepare his fellow citizens for their participation in the war against fascism and, later, to establish the United Nations. Chapter 8 tells the story of the development of rights discourse in the post-war United States, whilst Chapter 9 does the same for the UN, bringing out the similarities between the international discourse and the American one. Chapter 10 returns to the Japanese story in order to make clear the continuing pertinence of social differences to understanding the possibilities and tensions that currently and, as it happens, fortunately complicate the 'human rights project'. Chapter 11 begins by outlining the resistance to the problematising of economic and social inequality and therefore also to the broadening of the sphere of reciprocity that was represented by the conventional philosophical discussion of, or related to, human rights in the West in the first three post-war decades. It then moves on to describe the five major challenges to the exclusions from the circle of reciprocity that are currently embedded in contemporary human rights discourse. These challenges, made increasingly powerful by globalisation, add up to a demand for what I term a 'new universalism'. The chapter ends by showing how a positive response to these challenges has transformed the sociological approach to human rights from a scepticism to an enthusiasm, as exemplified by the reinvention of the principle of reciprocity to be found in the writings of contemporary sociologists. The Conclusion to the study as a whole returns to the issues raised by the paradoxical nature of human rights in the context of the difficulties and opportunities created by globalisation and the past history of rights discourse.

I

MAKING RIGHTS

1

THE PARADOX OF HUMAN RIGHTS

The two most general questions addressed in this study are:

How did human rights become entangled with power relations?

How might the nature of this entanglement be altered so that human rights may better serve the global majority?

In answering these questions, I will relate and indeed, in an analytical sense, subordinate the human rights story to the larger story of social change. For this reason, I will focus not so much on the history of the idea of human rights as on the social sources of this idea and, especially, on the concrete social activities or problems that rights have been developed to facilitate or solve, as well as on the equally concrete legal forms through which rights have been developed and attached to bearers in a diverse set of societies. This is primarily because, to develop the earlier point about the relationship between human rights regimes and the disposition of power, the existence of rights and, most importantly, any practical protective effectiveness they may have, represents the tip of a social iceberg. What I mean by this is that, other than in a limited but, as will be seen, nevertheless important legal sense, rights are neither self-generated nor self-enforcing, but rather summarise, make concrete, and depend for any protective effectiveness they may possess on, the nature of wider sets of social relations and developments within them. Thus the rights now identified as human rights were initially produced by national sets of social relations as a means of reinforcing a new mode of social discipline in a particular area of social life.

In other words, for me as a sociologist, rights, even human rights, are nothing special but simply a subset of a larger set of social relations that produce and enforce behavioural expectations, a subset distinguished by their legal form and their focus on the prevention of the abuse of power. That is, just as there is far more in rights than law alone, so for rights to work far more than law itself is required. Thus rights as such do not carry the whole or even much of the weight, so to speak, of ensuring that the pertinent social expectations are met but simply reinforce other means of preventing abuse or delivering entitlements. Indeed the presence of rights is therefore often a mark of some kind of social disruption, whether welcome or not, in that it indicates either that expectations have changed or that pre-existing or other methods of ensuring the meeting of such social expectations are no longer, or not yet, working effectively. The general point has been well made by Alasdair MacIntyre in a way that is directly relevant to the present study:

> Traditional European society inherited from the Greeks and from Christianity a moral vocabulary in which to judge an action good was to judge it to be the action of a good man, and to judge a man good was to judge him as manifesting dispositions (virtues) which enabled him to play a certain kind of role in a certain kind of social life . . . But the breakup of the traditional forms of social life which was produced by the rise of individualism, begotten partly by Protestantism and capitalism, made the reality of social life so different from the norms implied in the traditional vocabulary that all the links between duty and happiness were gradually broken. The consequence was a redefinition of moral terms. Happiness is no longer defined in terms of satisfactions which are understood in the light of the criteria governing a form of social life; it is defined in terms of individual psychology. Since such a psychology does not yet exist, it has to be invented. Hence the whole apparatus of appetites, passions, inclinations, *principles* [such as rights], which is found in every eighteenth century moral philosopher.
>
> (MacIntyre, 1967, p. 161, emphasis added)

By the same token, the absence of rights does not necessarily indicate that rights are needed since there may be no such disruption, and even if there is, it may not be of a kind that can be fixed by either legal innovation or the legal reinforcement of existing sets of social relations – if, for example, there is no 'liberty' in everyday life, no amount of human rights legislation will magic it into existence, with the result that other means of achieving the desired protections and/or delivering the deserved entitlements should be sought.

Given this basic stance, one might assume that a sociologist would argue that each society will exhibit the level of human rights protection it deserves – 'good societies' will exhibit high levels of protection, whilst 'bad societies' will exhibit low levels of protection. There is certainly a great deal of truth in such a proposition, but fortunately and unfortunately things are not so simple. What makes them not so simple is the fact that the inequalities intrinsic to even 'good societies' also, to varying degrees, affect the coverage, value content and legal form of their domestic rights discourses. The result is that, in the absence of a vigorously democratic culture (that is, under normal circumstances) and left to its own devices, each society will tend to produce a human rights regime that suits itself, especially in the sense that it interferes as little as possible with the prevailing disposition of power. Thus, although human rights regimes provide protections for the weaker parties in sets of social relations, there are always modes of protection available that are less disruptive of the status quo than others, and these less disruptive regimes are those that tend to become established. To take two extreme examples: in the United States the disposition of economic power is even more unequal than that of the other types of power with the result that economic and social rights are minimal as compared to civil and political rights; by contrast, in China the disposition of political power is even more unequal than that of the other types of power with the result that civil and political rights are minimal as compared to economic and social rights, or were until recently. And what makes things certainly not simple today is the fact that states are not left entirely to their own devices but are judged against the international standard represented by the UDHR and its related covenants. This standard represents the tip of another, but this time global, social iceberg. However, to complicate things even more, and this time reflecting the global disposition of power, this standard is primarily American in inspiration rather than truly cosmopolitan in the sense of being an authentically global product.

If one has doubts concerning the dependence of our current human rights regime on an hierarchical and more specifically American model, one has only to recognise two things. First, the image of the good or 'good enough' society projected by the UDHR corresponded remarkably closely at the time it was adopted to a then current idealised representation of the United States and a few other western societies rather than to a representation of, say, China. Second, the UDHR does not speak of the inherent equality of individual human beings but of their 'inherent dignity' – significantly to my mind, many a slave has been not only dignified but treated with dignity (Hindess and Hirst, 1977, pp. 116, 123–4). Thus Article 2 lists the types of person that the UDHR offers equal protection to as: people distinguished by 'race, colour, sex, language, religion, political or other opinion, national or social origin, property, birth or other status'. In other words, unlike slavery which is expressly forbidden (Article 4), hierarchies formed on such bases are deemed acceptable, provided only that the subordinated do not suffer the gross abuses itemised in the remainder of the UDHR. Moreover, the abuse one is protected against most often arises from the arbitrariness, or legally unsanctioned nature, of (on the original understanding) a state action rather than from the nature of the action itself. This is so even in the case of torture (Article 5) whose definition, as Talal Asad (1996, p. 1095) has shown, rests on a distinction between 'necessary suffering' and 'unnecessary suffering' that was developed in colonial settings and which singles out directly inflicted pain as far more reprehensible than, for example, any suffering or 'economic violence' caused by 'development' (Baxi, 2002, pp. 115–16; Rajagopal, 2003, pp. 182–3). Thus, although Article 3 declares that 'everyone has the right to life, liberty and the security of person', many of the subsequent articles make it clear that the state may deprive anyone of these rights, provided only that this is not done arbitrarily or with the use of directly inflicted pain. In other words, the UDHR in no way reduces the inequality of power between the state and the citizen but instead, in the name of the limited form of reciprocity summarised by the term human dignity, imposes some limits on the possible consequences of such inequality by insisting that the state as well as the citizenry should be subject to the rule of law.

The only other limitations on the possible consequences of the inequality between the state and the citizen specified in the UDHR are the indirect ones represented by: 'the right to take part in the government of . . . [one's] country' (Article 21); and 'the right to seek and to enjoy in other countries asylum from persecution' (Article 14). As Susan Marks (2000) has shown, Article 21 has typically been interpreted in the narrowest and most formal way possible so that it refers to little more than a way of choosing leaders. And Article 14 both confirms the limited nature of all the other constraints on the state by advising flight as the only reliable means of self-protection and imposes all the costs (especially the psychological ones) of so extreme a measure on the individual, unless the receiving state, as it should, provides some help. Finally and similarly, even the small number of economic and social rights included in the UDHR – to social security, work, protection against unemployment, non-discrimination in employment, 'just and favourable remuneration', trade union membership, rest and leisure, and education – are intended only to limit or ameliorate the effects of economic and social inequality rather than do anything about these forms of inequality as such.

One consequence of the American influence on international human rights discourse is that it currently seems very unlikely that the United States will ever be formally judged against standards other than its own. Thus, despite being central to, and indeed predominant within, the global system in many other ways, the United States will continue to be left to its own devices in the sphere of human rights. Another and contrasting consequence is that much of the rest of the world finds itself caught in a vicious circle. On the one hand, the more different a society is as compared to the United States, the more likely it is to be regarded as providing a low level of human rights protection. On the other hand, no matter how enthusiastically the American-inspired regime may be adopted, it is unlikely ever to become embedded deeply enough in the social routines of non-American locations to represent an effective means of countering abuse within them. Thus, if things remain as they are, the net result as regards the future is not encouraging in that levels of human rights abuse in the United States as well as the rest of the world will, at best, continue at their present levels or, more likely, increase.

A sociological approach to my question as to how human rights became entangled with power relations leads, then, to the exposure of a self-regarding American or more broadly western localism where a tran-scendental universalism has otherwise been assumed. This is because a sociological approach refuses to separate rights from social life as a whole and issues of power in particular, and as a result insists on problematising the claims to equality made in the name of human rights both nationally and internationally. A sociological approach also points to an ambivalent answer to my question as to how the nature of this entanglement might be altered so that human rights may better serve the global majority. In this case not so much because what had been assumed to be universal values turn out to be in fact ethnocentric, but for the deeper reason that the historical emergence of the very idea of human sacredness, on which that of human rights depends even if it was not directly derived from it, was coterminous with the emergence of what are commonly referred to as structural inequalities – that is, with the emergence of forms of inequality that are independent of personal attributes and instead derive from modes of economic, political and cultural organisation. Prior to the emergence of such inequalities and therefore within what have been variously referred to as tribal, stateless, 'primitive communist', autochthonous, or *chthonic* societies, there were few if any acts that one would recognise today as human rights violations. This was because the reciprocal interdependence of group members, the related absences of anything like a state and any idea of property made each member equally necessary to the group's survival and therefore equally precious despite, or, better, because of, the additional absence of any notion of individuality.

When viewed sociologically, then, the present prominence accorded human rights should inspire in western opinion not complacency let alone pride, but instead a scepticism and a profound sense of cultural humility; if, that is, one is looking for a practical and effective global ethic that both universally limits abuse and encapsulates the moral wisdom of the human species as whole rather than simply generalises the ethic of a sub-species that has only recently appeared and which we might call *Homo americanus*. More particularly, scepticism and humility are appropriate because, in sociologically understanding human rights, we must somehow wean ourselves from the comforting contractarian myth that rights are part of our primordial inheritance. Instead, we must come to terms with the much less comfortable fact that the critical moment in the development of both the idea of human sacredness and the power to violate this sacred character legitimately (that is, in the name of the state) was everywhere one and the same, namely that on which the practice of human sacrifice was initiated.

HUMAN SACRIFICE AND HUMAN RIGHTS

Thus, *if* one wanted to locate a remote origin for the idea that it would be socially benefical to specify and institutionalise a set of inviolable human rights, a much more plausible candidate than some imagined and retrojected social contract is available. To develop the point, this more plausible candidate is that represented by all those real, apparently universal, and indeed good faith efforts to render the individual human being sacred which occurred whenever some powerful people decided both to regulate the killing of individuals and to please or placate the gods by sacrificing an innocent but less powerful person as a surrogate for a more obvious candidate, namely the 'king'. Human sacrifice rendered the individual human life sacred (as an appropriate offering), but at the same time obscured the fact that the social inequalities that made such sacrifice possible were sacrilised too (as a cause worthy of the gods' favours). Also, the necessity of sacrifice was presented, and very likely experienced, as required by the principle of reciprocity that was commonly supposed to govern social life; that is, the victim believed that he or she owed his or her life to the gods, so it seemed only right that their life should be returned to the gods when the latter appeared to deserve or need it (Agamben, 1998; Bataille, 1973, pp. 59–61; Carter, 2003; Hubert and Mauss, 1979; Girard, 1979, 1994).

Whether or not there is any kind of direct link, it is possible to see a clear analogical link between rights and human sacrifice. Thus, to anticipate the argument to come, just as human sacrifice made sacred both the individual human being and the inequalities that made sacrifice possible, so the sacrifices required by an emergent capitalism made sacred both certain aspects of the individual life as god-given, 'natural' rights and the inequalities that made the same capitalism possible. In other words, both 'natural' rights and human sacrifice are instances of unequal rather than equal exchange. Likewise, in both cases the victim's acceptance of their fate was a consequence of their participation in the routine activities and beliefs of their society. More specifically, in the case of 'natural' rights, what was made sacred was not the whole person but rather certain aspects of their lives – the freedoms to own property in the means of production, to work, and make contracts, for example – as well as, of course, capitalist production relations in general. And the major sacrifice was, again, not of whole human beings but of other aspects of their lives such as their labour power and therefore any expectation of economic security. Thus 'natural' rights, like the rites associated with human sacrifice, represent an assertion of state power rather than an antidote to it with the result that the protections and/or support they promise come at a price.

Though seldom made manifest, this insight has long been latent in sociology, as is illustrated by Karl Marx's, admittedly passing, references to human sacrifice when he speaks of the fate of the unemployed under capitalism in *Capital* I. In a far more elaborate form, it is also present in the combination of Marx's understanding that rights came into existence because 'commodities cannot take themselves to market' (see below, p. 21) and Georg Lukacs' Weberian development of Marx's concept of alienation to provide an account of 'reification'; that is, of what happens to labour power when it is taken to market by its supposedly rightful individual owners:

> the worker . . . is the victim . . . [cut off] from his labour power . . . [and] . . . by selling this, his only commodity, [the worker] . . . integrates it (and himself: for his commodity is inseparable from his physical existence) into a specialized process that has been rationalized and mechanized, a process that he discovers already existing, complete

> and able to function without him and in which he is no more than a
> cipher reduced to an abstract quantity, a mechanized and rationalized
> tool.
>
> (Lukacs, 1922, pp. 165–6)

Moreover, Lukacs, following Marx more strictly in this instance, goes on to point out that the sacrifice of labour power is most often presented and experienced not as an imposition but as required by the same principle of mutually beneficial, reciprocal exchange as supposedly governs the society as a whole – workers owe their lives to participation in exchange relations so it seems only right that they should exchange part of themselves too. In a formulation that again but less directly evokes the trope of human sacrifice, Marx (1871) draws an analogy from the 'mist-enveloped regions of the religious world' and refers to this phase of the process as a consequence of 'the fetishism of commodities'.

Insofar as our contemporary discourse of human rights incorporates the original set of civil rights, the figure of human sacrifice remains apt as a means of summarising and shaping the way we should understand the nature of human rights. Moreover, although our contemporary discourse sacrilises a wider array of human attributes or requirements – in this case not through, but as an act of atonement for, the mass killing of innocents by the Nazis – in so doing it continues to obscure the importance of some of the inequalities – notably the economic inequalities – that made Nazism possible. This is not simply because human rights discourse is a continuation of plain rights discourse wherein the privileging of private property is obscured by the apparent reciprocity of the market. It is also because the UDHR is informed by an understanding of the causes of fascism that stresses civil and political rather than economic and social factors (Morsink, 1999, ch. 1; for an alternative understanding, see Poulantzas, 1974). In sum, for me, human sacrifice represents the *ur* form of what might be called the 'human rights paradox': human rights are intended to protect potential victims by declaring aspects of their lives sacred, but they also contribute to the continuation of the possibility of abuse by protecting some of the activities that give rise to the same abuse. Thus human rights discourse was not constructed on the basis of the value of reciprocity, but instead on the bases of the dominance of the value of autonomy over that of reciprocity with result that it does not address the deeper causes of such abuse but simply suggests some means for managing and limiting its nature and frequency.

Three consequences follow from locating the study of human rights within the framework represented by the ambivalent figure of human sacrifice.[1] First, any history of human rights produced within it will look markedly less positive than those produced within a conventional social contract framework since it will be a story of loss, lack and privilege as well as of gain, recognition and justice. Second, respect for human rights cannot logically result in the end of inequality since human rights as an idea, let alone a disciplinary practice, is only possible because of the inequalities intrinsic to the existence of the state and capitalism. Hence, if one wished to prevent rather than simply limit and manage human rights abuses, a much broader and indeed very different strategy would be required since it is these underlying inequalities that would have to be addressed. Third, the differences between rights regimes arise because the level and type of abuses tolerated within particular societies or globally are understood to vary not simply with the level of autonomy allowed to individuals, as many contractarians would have it, but also with the balance between this autonomy and the forms and degrees of reciprocity that are part of the state's package of compensations for its assumption of power over life and death.

RECIPROCITY, AUTONOMY AND HUMAN RIGHTS

The significance of these consequences will become apparent as the study proceeds. This said, it is necessary at this point to elaborate a little on the third of these conclusions. To my legally, but in no other sense, positivist mind, rights are simply 'socially determined policy objectives' (Hirst, 1979, p. 104), which means that their existence does not require justification so much as explanation. For this reason, Immanuel Kant's natural law ethics might seem an inappropriate place for me to begin my substantive argument. However, Kant's ideas are generally thought to have been or, at least, to have become, the basis for the range of 'socially determined policy objectives' specified in the UDHR. Thus, both because of their practical social significance and for rhetorical reasons, I have derived my sense of the importance of the balance between autonomy and reciprocity not just from rethinking human rights through the figure of human sacrifice but also from reconsidering Kant's concepts of 'republicanism' and 'cosmopolitanism'.

In line with my reconstructive agenda concerning human rights, the rhetorical effect I seek is both critical and recuperative. Today, Kant is most often presented as an unqualified supporter, *avant la lettre* of course, of the conventional understanding of human rights. Indeed, it is commonly argued that his concept of autonomy specifies the very essence of human rights. For Kant, autonomy refers to the human individual's capacity to reflect on the world and, on this basis, decide how to act. The possession of this capacity, and as importantly, its uniqueness in nature, defines the core of both what it means to be human and the ethic that republicanism should aspire to realise. Thus, even under a highly developed form of republicanism, where social contract theory commands general assent, and where liberty, popular sovereignty, and the rule of law are established, only 'active' citizens (that is, independent property owners rather than, for example, journeymen, domestic tutors, women or state dependants) are deemed to possess the autonomy necessary to qualify as voters. Nevertheless, the remainder of the citizenry (that is, the journeymen etc.) have the right to expect that their 'active' brethren will nevertheless recognise their reciprocal obligations to those who serve or depend on them by, for example, paying taxes: '[f]or the general will of the people has united to form a society which must constantly maintain itself, and to this end, it has subjected itself to the internal power of the state so as to preserve those . . . who cannot do so themselves' (Kant, 1797, reprinted in Ishay, 1997, p. 163).

Moreover, at the international level an even larger role is played by the principle of reciprocity. This is because it is central to the cosmopolitanism Kant deploys in order to define the basis on which states, republican or otherwise, might be brought to live in peace with one another rather than engage in war and conquest. This cosmopolitanism is rooted in the recognition that 'originally' there was no collective let alone individual ownership:

> The rational idea . . . of a *peaceful* (if not exactly amiable) international community . . . is not a philanthropic principle of ethics, but a principle of *right* . . . [A]ll nations are *originally* members of a community of the land. But this is not a legal community of possession (*communio*) and utilisation of the land, nor a community of ownership. It is a community of <u>reciprocal action</u> (*commercium*) . . . and each member of it accordingly has constant relations with all the others . . . This right in so far as it affords the prospect that all nations may unite for the purpose of creating certain universal laws to regulate the intercourse they may have with one another, may be termed *cosmopolitan* (*ius cosmopoliticum*).
>
> (ibid., p. 171, underlining added, emphasis in original)

Kant himself, unlike many of his more recent readers (Held, 1997, 2004, pp. 170–8; Ignatieff, 2001, for example), who appear to think of cosmopolitanism as autonomy writ global, was very aware of the continuing importance of reciprocity and consequently of the difference and therefore the tension between an ethics of republicanism and an ethics of cosmopolitanism. On the one hand, Kant argues for the spread of republicanism and strongly counsels against even political let alone economic revolution. But, on the other hand, he equally strongly argues against colonialism and insists that any cosmopolitan constitution 'must not simply be derived from the experience of those who have hitherto fared best under it' (Kant, 1797, reprinted in Ishay, 1997, p. 173). On my reading, and prompted by John Rawls' (1999) Kant-inspired argument in *The Law of the Peoples*, this suggests that any cosmopolitan constitutional element such as that represented by human rights cannot be derived simply from the principle of autonomy, but must also acknowledge non-republican traditions and therefore find room for the principle of reciprocity. In sum, for Kant the reason why reciprocity, its forms, and the balance between it and autonomy matter is because reciprocity is the most basic condition of sociability, both nationally and internationally, and is therefore simultaneously a prerequisite for individual autonomy and a constraint upon it (for the sociological rediscovery of this understanding, see below, p. 47, 128–34).

The practical significance of Kant's cosmopolitanism is that it specifies what one is looking for in any putative global ethic – hence the importance of what one understands it to be. Thus, on my reading at least, one must judge any extant or proposed human rights regime according to the richness or otherwise of the mixture of elements favouring autonomy or reciprocity that it contains: an unbalanced mixture suggests distance from even its avowed ideal and therefore an increased danger of abuse, whilst a balanced mixture suggests closeness to the ideal. It is, then, the unbalanced nature of the current human rights regime (elements favouring autonomy far outweigh those favouring reciprocity both in terms of perceived significance and quantity) that ultimately causes me not only to judge it to rest on a thin variant of the principle of reciprocity but also to judge it as embodying an exclusionary conception of autonomy (cp. Glendon, 1996; Gutman, 2001).

This said, my earlier reading of the UDHR may have seemed excessively negative, and so it was. Given the extent of the inequalities whose consequences the UDHR seeks to qualify and the implacability of the global structural forces – summarised by the terms 'state' and 'capitalism' – that have produced these inequalities, it is remarkable that even the slight and unreliable protections listed in the UDHR are available at all. Thus we have every reason to be grateful for the limits on their own power acknowledged by those who first rendered human life sacred by sacrificing some of their people. Of course, those of us who might otherwise have been amongst the sacrificial victims have even more reason to be grateful to those who, over several millennia and in many different ways in different parts of the world, developed metaphorical stories such as those concerning Christ's crucifixion and resurrection as well as surrogate sacrificial rituals such as Holy Communion, that also sacrilise human life but without requiring anyone to die (Ishay, 1997, ch. 1). And, finally, we in the contemporary West have particular reason to be grateful to those who, over the past 200 or so years, have resisted the state and capital and in so doing turned the presumption of sacredness into the specific and concrete protections assembled in national constitutions, bodies of statutory and case law, the various UN covenants, conventions, or treaties, and often, as well as most significantly, embedded in the routine practices of governments, armies, police forces and employers.

Nonetheless, I have stressed the negative for three main reasons. First, it illustrates the difference made by looking at human rights sociologically. Second, it is not done often enough with the result that, for the reasons set out by Stanley Cohen (2000), denial and/or complacency reign where anger and desire should still be – in our hearts (see below, p. 134). Third, it suggests what has to be done if human rights are to be made into a more effective mode of protection and support even within their restricted ambit of concerns. To elaborate on the last reason, my earlier point about rights regimes tending to follow the line of least resistance in relation to the disposition of power (see above, p. 5) implies the following: first, given the variations in rights discourses consequent upon social-structural differences, a properly cosmopolitan rights regime would show up the gaps and weaknesses in particular national regimes; and second, since simply transplanting the missing rights from one location to another is unlikely to work because of the social equivalent of 'organ rejection' in transplant surgery, those charged with the task of developing and enforcing human rights will have to be creative in finding ways of using the existing limited resources to fill the gaps in ways that are embeddable within the societies of concern (for some suggestions as to how this might be done, see Woodiwiss, 2003). Thus, as an example, although American workers clearly lack economic rights as compared to their Japanese opposite numbers, it seems much more likely that they would see enhanced organising and bargaining rights as more acceptable than an offer of Japanese-style 'lifetime employment' as a means of recognising their need.

In conclusion, the human rights story will not be presented here in the conventional manner as the supposedly linear and inherently progressive history of an *idea* from ancient times, through such texts as Magna Carta (1215), the English Bill of Rights (1688), Locke's *Second Treatise on*

Civil Government (1689), the Habeas Corpus Acts (1692), the great French (1789) and American (1791) declarations of rights, to the UDHR (1948). Rather, the story will be told as an aspect of a larger story of social change and the replacement of old by new inequalities, as a matter of the legal technology developed in the context of these more general changes, and more substantively as involving the gradual, but I hope temporary, displacement of reciprocity by autonomy at the core of the discourse. As will quickly become apparent, telling the story in this way transforms not simply the significance of the texts that are emphasised in the conventional accounts and the chronological occasion of their influence, but also the meaning of the whole enterprise. Thus, to simplify: whereas the conventional account presents the first chapter of the story as beginning with freedom and ending with private property, the sociological account reverses this chronology; and, more generally, whereas conventional analysis presents rights as simply a defence against power, the sociological account presents rights as also a product of power.

One result of these analytical differences is that many of especially the earlier texts central to the conventional story turn out to be important not so much as sources of inspiration or visions but more as *post factum* rationalisations of a much later and, for many, far from inspirational set of developments. Magna Carta provides the most obvious example in that it did not become a significant text in the history of rights until Sir Edward Coke opportunistically invoked it as a justification for the then emergent capitalist property right in the early seventeenth century (see below, p. 35). When viewed sociologically, then, rights discourse does not refer to a set of inspirational transcendental principles that has lead us to the good society. It refers instead to a set of practical means of self and social-protection that, despite a somewhat suspect provenance, has nevertheless sometimes and in some places been highly effective in protecting some people. The appropriate way to approach human rights, therefore, is neither reverently nor dismissively but practically and with a view to understanding how they have worked for some and might be yet be made to work for all.

2

TOWARDS A SOCIOLOGY OF RIGHTS

This chapter focuses on the development of sociological thinking concerning the reasons why, first, legal and, latterly, moral discourse took the form of an increasingly coherent system of rights in the course of the transition from feudalism to capitalism. The following chapter uses these sociological ideas to look more closely at what is an especially pertinent segment of the larger story told in the present chapter, namely that concerning how some amongst the larger system of rights were singled out as natural rights and in this way turned into the core of the system. The analytical point of these chapters is twofold. One, self-evidently, is to introduce the approach taken by sociologists to the study of rights. The other, perhaps less obviously, is to make clear from the beginning the specificity and complexity of the set of social relations that both the general idea of rights and what are commonly considered to be the core civil rights were part of as they emerged. The latter point will have a significant bearing on the approach I will take in subsequent chapters to the issue of the universality or otherwise of today's array of human rights.

Before one can talk of anything in any culture as a precursor of our human rights construct, that culture has to have also produced a conception of persons as individuals and/or members of groups, a state, and a legal system capable of enforcing any limitations or requirements that might be applicable (cp. Galtung, 1994). Although it was undoubtedly not the first culture where a conception of an individual as a person or member of a legally recognised group, a state, and an effective legal system were present, it is clear that, in the West at least, the most influential such culture was that of Rome. What we now call, perhaps too casually, 'Roman law' recognised individuals in so far as it enabled them to preserve and protect their portions of their nevertheless still conjoint or 'bilateral' interests in and *vis-à-vis* things owned and exchanged (Glenn, 2000, pp. 119–20). The manner in which such regulation was achieved did not involve a rights construct, since the interests of concern were not 'formulated as unilateral [individualised] entitlements' (ibid., p. 130). However, its formulation and administration were entrusted by the Roman state to experts – *iudices* (judges) and *praetors* (lawyers) – who were enjoined to act rationally, and whose decisions were ultimately recorded in systematic way as a *codex (code)*, such as *The Digest of Justinian* (ibid., pp. 118–20). Through the survival of such codes, and indeed their use within Christian canon law (Berman, 1994), but of course completely unintentionally, a legal simulacrum of an idealised, interdependent communal life remained available long after the real thing had disappeared and as western European society became ever more unequal and its law gradually became increasingly individualised.

In this way, then, and because of the preservation, often thanks to Arab libraries as well as Christian monasteries, of many of the pertinent Roman texts, rights as individualised entitlements were made both technically possible for, and socially meaningful and acceptable to, later generations of western Europeans. That is, Roman law made it possible more than a thousand years after its demise for Jurists to begin to think that individuals were entitled to have and protect their own unilateral interests, since in the end they remained parts of a larger interdependent and therefore reciprocally dependent whole. Initially, this larger whole was understood to derive from the god-given natural law and latterly to derive from the results of the secular reasoning summarised in the form of either the codes of the continental civil law tradition or the textbooks of the Anglo-American common law tradition. An important step in this process took the form of a wonderfully bizarre inversion in that the systematicity of Roman law, which arose from it 'look[ing] like life' (ibid., p. 119), ultimately allowed the thought that humanity's original condition had been an individualised one. That is, it made it possible for certain adherents to social contract theory, notably William Blackstone (see below, p. 37), to argue that since social order was a mark of development, it must have been preceded by the chaos of freedom! This inversion was the one that singled out certain civil rights (to own property, work and make contracts), privileged them as the premier natural rights, and thereby ultimately legitimised the ever increasing inequality produced by the emerging capitalism. But why and how was it that these particular rights were chosen? To answer the why question, I will now outline some of the more influential answers provided by social theorists. In the following chapter, I will answer the how question by applying these theorists' ideas to the development of rights in English and American legal and political discourse up to the beginning of the nineteenth century.

There is a one-word answer to the why question – capitalism. To justify this answer requires the use of rather more words since the relationship between the development of capitalism and the increasing importance of the law and therefore rights was one of the principal preoccupations of the classical sociologists. Marx and Engels wrote a great deal about the nature of law, although not as much as about the law's relation to the wider society, whether feudal or capitalist (Cain and Hunt, 1979). Of the many points they made, two appear to have been the most influential. Both, not surprisingly, were very general and therefore required considerable critical elaboration before anything like an adequate understanding of the relationship between the development of capitalism and the increasing role of the law could be derived from them. The first was that the institutions of the law were elements of the state structure and, because for Marx the state is but the 'executive committee of the bourgeoisie', legal institutions were used by the latter to advance their interests. The second was that legal concepts were ideological categories and, because for Marx 'the ruling ideas of a period are in every epoch the ideas of the ruling class', the use of these concepts caused people both to think about their behaviour and act in terms that, again, advanced the interests of the bourgeoisie. Neither of these ideas was applied to the law in any systematic way until the 1920s when the Austrian social-democrat and future Chancellor, Karl Renner, applied the first in his *The Institutions of the Private Law and their Social Function*, and the Bolshevik intellectual and future victim of Stalin's purges, Evgeny Pashukanis, applied the second in his *Law and Marxism: a General Theory*.

RENNER: LAW, STATE AND PRODUCTION

Renner's core idea was that, although the formal legal categories, including the general idea of rights, were in themselves abstract and neutral, their deployment by the state at the behest of the bourgeoisie meant that their content corresponded to the latter's interests and changed with these interests. Thus he argued that the basic elements of what was to become bourgeois law reflected the requirements of the earliest widespread form of commodity production, namely simple or petty commodity production.

This is independent production for sale without the use of wage-labour and is most often exemplified by the family farm or the artisan's workshop. With the subsequent rise of capitalism, especially factory capitalism, Renner argued that these basic elements had their content changed to suit the new demands of capitalist commodity producers. The main points made in the course of Renner's historico-sociological analysis are concisely summarised in the following extract from Otto Kahn-Freund's introduction to the English translation of Renner's book:

> Property, then, the central institution of private law, fulfilled, in the system of simple commodity production, the functions of providing an order of goods, and, in part, an order of power. It did so without any essential aid from other institutions. It was not, however, able, to guarantee for any length of time an order of labour. Outside labour was increasingly used by the independent artisans, and this was regulated not by the law of property itself, but by complementary norms, norms which were at first derived from public gild law, and subsequently from the law of free employment. It is at this point that the order of simple commodity production starts to break up, and the functional transformation of private law, and of the law of property in particular, begins.
>
> The law of property was substantially the same in 1900 as in 1600, but what had become of its social functions? Did it still provide an order of production? No: the producer now worked in another man's house, with another man's tools. The producer was still the detentor of the raw materials, the means of production, the finished products, but they were no longer 'his'. Ownership was no longer capable of expressing the order of goods.
>
> Did it, then, fulfil its function to regulate consumption?
>
> No, the man still 'occupied' the house in which he lived, but he occupied it as a tenant. The furniture which he 'held' and used was, perhaps, hired under a hire-purchase contract. The house, the family, had long ceased to be a universal unit of consumption. The children were educated in schools, the sick cared for in hospitals, the old and invalid in homes.
>
> The *universitas rerum* of the 'house', that microcosm of tangible objects which had been the substratum of the property norm, had been torn asunder, but the norm survived the destruction of its substratum. The single pieces – things – which had been the constituting elements of a functional entity had been – in the Marxist sense – 'expropriated'. Each object – land, house, means of production, commodities for consumption – followed its own destiny.

> The things which a man owns are no longer held together by a common function. Nothing except the fact of ownership itself links them together. If and in so far as, they are consumers' goods – a dwelling house and garden, an allotment, furniture etc. – they 'belong' to their owner not only in the legal, but also in the functional sense. But the bulk of all the things which are privately owned have no intrinsic connection with the proprietor at all. They happen to belong to him – legally – they would function just as well if they belonged to someone else. From his point of view their sole object is to be a title, to profits, a title to interest, a title to rent . . . The property object has become capital.
>
> (Renner, 1949, pp. 26–7)

In short, the concept of private property was initially very broad. If one owned one's own house/workshop, one could determine: (a) what should be produced; (b) how labour could be deployed; and c) how any surplus created should be consumed. As a result, in Renner's terms, the concept of private property contained an 'order of power', an 'order of labour', and an 'order of goods'. Subsequently, however and as capitalism developed, the rights distinguished in relation to the concept of property were gradually restricted so that eventually, on its own, it simply allowed the owners of means of production to appropriate any profit produced as a result of their use. It ceased to define an order of labour since for this a contract of employment was required, albeit initially of a simple oral kind. Nor did it define an order of goods since it was gradually left to wage-earners themselves and the state to determine how goods should be consumed. In this way, then, Renner argued that law as a 'common will' imposed by the state changed as the forms of production changed in an 'evolutionary' and 'organic' way, but with increasingly positive support from the state (ibid., pp. 45–8, 292–8). The state therefore mediated between the economy and the law, so that those who dominated the economy, controlled the state and determined the content of the law, which in turn regulated an economy of individuals, supposedly in the interests of the whole community.

PASHUKANIS: LAW, IDEOLOGY AND THE MARKET

Pashukanis found little to disagree with in Renner's understanding of the relationship between the development of capitalism and the increasing importance of the law except for Renner's assumption that legal categories, notably rights, were in themselves neutral containers, which only served the bourgeoisie because of the context in which they were produced and the content that was therefore given to them. Pashukanis shared Marx's conviction as to whose progeny the ruling ideas of a period were. At the centre of his work was Marx's concept of fetishism, as is apparent in this outline of its main thesis:

> Whereas the commodity acquires its value independently of the will of the producing subject, the realisation of its value in the process of exchange presupposes a conscious act of will on the part of the owner of the commodity, or as Marx says:
>
> > Commodities cannot themselves go to market and perform exchange in their own right. We must, therefore, have recourse to their guardians, who are the possessors of commodities. Commodities are things, and therefore lack the power to resist man. If they are unwilling, he can use force; in other words, he can take possession of them.
> >
> > It follows that the necessary condition for the realisation of the social link between people in the production process – reified in the products of labour and disguised as an elementary category (*Gesetzmassigkeit*) – is a particular relationship between people with products at their disposal, or subjects whose 'will resides in those objects'.

That goods contain labour is one of their intrinsic qualities; that they are exchangeable is a distinct quality, one solely dependent on the will of the possessor, and one which presupposes that they are owned and alienable.

At the same time, therefore, that the product of labour becomes a commodity and a bearer of value, a man acquires the capacity to be a legal subject and a bearer of rights. The person whose will is declared as decisive is the legal subject . . .

If objects dominate man economically because, as commodities, they embody a social relation which is not subordinate to man, then man rules over things legally, because, in his capacity as possessor and proprietor, he is simply the personification of the abstract, impersonal, legal subject, the pure product of social relations, in Marx's words:

> In order that these objects may enter into relations with each other as commodities, their guardians must place themselves in relation to one another as persons whose will resides in those objects, and

> must behave in such a way that each does not appropriate the
> commodity of the other, and alienate his own, except through an act
> to which both parties consent. The guardians must therefore
> recognise each other as owners of private property.
>
> (Pashukanis, 1978, pp. 112–14)

For Pashukanis, then, the origin of the category of rights was neither
abstract reasoning nor some primordial social contract, as it had been
for the simultaneously emerging liberal jurisprudence, but rather the
emergence of a need to find an appropriate way to think about and regulate
commodity production as a social process in order that surplus value may
be produced, realised as profit and accumulated as capital. The conclusion
he drew from this was that all legal concepts based upon and articulating
rights were intrinsically bourgeois. More radically still, he argued that
insofar as rights are constitutive of law then law in itself is inherently
bourgeois and should therefore have no place in a future communist
society.

WEBER, DURKHEIM AND THE INTERNAL LIFE OF THE LAW

The other two members of sociology's founding triumvirate, Max Weber
and Emile Durkheim, took the law and rights far more seriously than Marx
and his followers. Far too seriously for Pashukanis who felt that Renner's
view as to the social neutrality of such legal categories as rights owed
something to Weber's 'bourgeois' thought. Thus the general significance
of Weber and Durkheim's contributions to the sociological understanding
of rights is not simply confirmation of the grounding of rights in the rise
of capitalism but, more distinctively, the beginnings of a more positive
assessment of their social significance. Weber and Durkheim's more specific
pertinences in the present context are that Weber solved the problem as
to how the common law managed to make itself appear coherent despite
its rejection of codification, whilst Durkheim took a surprisingly close
interest in the specific role of the changing relationships between property
and contract in English law in defining what might be called the emerging
inner morality of the law, namely the 'organic solidarity' that he imagined
would be characteristic of post-capitalist societies exhibiting a highly
elaborated and non-pathological division of labour. More specifically,
Durkheim was interested in the way in which, despite its capitalist
associations, the gradual displacement of property by contract represented
a prefiguration of a new and egalitarian moral community. Thus there
are important things to be learnt from the discussions of the histories

of 'property' and 'contract' contained in *Professional Ethics and Civic Morals* (1957: for unknowing empirical confirmation of Durkheim's analysis, see Atiyah, 1979, pp. 85–90, 102–12).

According to Durkheim, something very significant happened to the meaning of 'property' in theory during the seventeenth century and in practice during the nineteenth. In the seventeenth century Locke propounded the theory, later accepted by Adam Smith, that property is only legitimate if it is founded on labour. In the nineteenth century the emergence of the 'will theory of contract' was both made possible and, as has been explained in some detail elsewhere (Woodiwiss, 1990b, Ch. 2), confirmed by this development:

> the bond of contract could not have had a very early origin. Indeed, men's wills cannot agree to contract obligations if these obligations do not arise from a status in law already acquired, whether of things or of persons; it can only be a matter of modifying the status and of superimposing new relations on those already existing. The contract, then, is a source of variations which presupposes a primary basis in law, but one that has a different origin. The contract is the supreme instrument by which transfers of ownership are carried through. The contract itself cannot constitute the primary foundations on which the right of contract rests. It implies that two legal entities at least are already properly constituted and of due capacity, that they enter into relations and that these relations change their constitution; that some thing belonging to the one passes to the other and vice versa.
>
> (Durkheim in Lukes and Scull, 1983, p. 194)

The point to be taken here from this passage and from Durkheim's discussion of contract in general is that it was only with the emergence of contract, and of the contract of employment in particular, that capitalism's exploitative production relations (instances of the 'forced division of labour' for Durkheim, 1964, pp. 374–88) became possible objects of reference for the legal system, and that the law of the market also became the law of production whether one is talking about the common or civil law systems (cp. Fox, 1974, pp. 188–9). To elaborate somewhat, what we now call 'private property' gradually emerged from the twelfth century onwards as a form of legal ownership distinguishable from feudal landholding or 'dominium' whereby land was held in the name of God and/or the monarch (Milsom, 1981, pp. 99 ff.). However, it was only in the nineteenth century that this process eventuated in the appearance of a specifically capitalist concept of private property thanks to the creation in law of the contract of employment, which belatedly recognised the social dominance of capitalist production relations relative to those of feudalism and simple commodity production. In sum, what one learns from Durkheim is that the development of the law of contract contributed to an equalisation of status in so far as everyone, whether property-holder or not, became a potential or actual contractor, and therefore a maker of social relations. In this way, not only was the legitimacy of capitalism secured for the time being, but also, for Durkheim, it became possible to imagine capitalism's possible supersession in that all aspects of the capital/labour relation as well as of many other social relations, could potentially be made subject to negotiation and/or legislation.

The appearance of a specifically capitalist concept of private property was also the development that finally enabled the common law to cease its hitherto total dependence on reasoning by analogy or what Weber (1978, pp. 655–6) termed 'merely paratactic association'. Thereafter, to use some additional Weberian terminology, the adepts of the common law commenced to deploy in their textbooks and elsewhere, the much more powerful techniques of 'synthetic construction' that had resulted in the 'systematisation' that characterised the continental codes (van Caenegem, 1992, ch. 2) and so produced images both of an apparently coherent legal discourse depicting a supposedly already just world and of themselves as an almost priestly caste possessed of the secret knowledge of its workings.

Putting the point less abstractly, rights as they emerged were understood both by contemporaries and by the classical sociological theorists as simply statements of correct practice ('objective right' within the Continental tradition) within a problem-solving discourse. The common law, for example, grew out of the 'unsystematised' (in Weber's sense) but clearly instrumental 'forms of action' or writs that Frederic William Maitland (1936) latterly studied (Milsom, 1981, pp. xxv ff.). For this reason, the law's initial content largely and predictably corresponded to the requirements of those who made demands upon the law, and, insofar as these tended to come from the propertied classes, these classes determined its content. However, as such discursive elements as 'property' and 'contract' became disarticulated from those that had initially expressed the claims of the feudal or 'landlord state', as they accumulated their own sets of treatises and case law, they gradually and unevenly attained a systematicity, an abstractness, and therefore an autonomy, not only from the claims of the anyway increasingly representative and in a sense plural state, but also from the claims that lay behind the proto-capitalist demands for legal redress which had initiated their disarticulation. In this way, then, rights became things in themselves that could be attached to individuals ('subjective right' in the Continental tradition).

ELIAS AND THE EMPOWERING OF THE LAW

Whilst, to my mind at least, the classical theorists established that the development of capitalism, the emergence of its class system, and the rise of a rights-based legal discourse were interlinked with one another, they did not specifically explain how the law came to have the power to operate as an effective disciplinary force in society. For an understanding of this process, we have to turn to the work of later generations of historico-sociological theorists and specifically that of Norbert Elias and Michel Foucault. Although he does not directly address the issue, much of what Elias argues in a work first published in German in 1939, *The Civilising Process* (1978a and b), is relevant to understanding the empowering of the law as a positive legal force. The most pertinent aspects of what is a very wide-ranging argument are fourfold and concern how it was possible that the law became an effective mode of social discipline. First, there is Elias' detailed elaboration of Weber's point about one of the distinctive features of the state in capitalist societies being its possession of a monopoly of legitimate physical force in its territory. Thus what Elias describes is the process through which the disarming of non-state forces and a huge growth, therefore, in the state's capacity to enforce its will was achieved in the course of the transition between feudalism and capitalism, whether legally mediated or not; that is, simply because the still-monarchical state's subjects were progressively denied access to the means to resist. Second, there is his complementary point concerning the reinforcement of the decline of violence in everyday life that followed from the disarmament of the general population by the redirecting of the nevertheless persisting aggressive impulses of the military caste into the safer channels represented by practices such as competitive displays of courtly manners, which required high degrees of self-control, and, to use an unusually apt present-day term, 'blood sports', which provided a legitimate outlet for any residual aggression. Later, a similar redirection of the aggressive impulses of the remainder of the population was achieved through the general diffusion of elaborate codes of manners and the creation of competitive sports. Third, both the arming of the state and the establishment and maintenance of royal courts that could administer, legally or otherwise, the pacified population and provide suitable venues for courtly display were made possible by the state's simultaneously developing monopolisation of taxation. Finally, Elias summarises the causes and consequences of the first three developments by reworking Durkheim's concept of the emergence of a new type of social solidarity – organic solidarity – understanding it as the product of ever longer 'chains of social interdependency'. Given the presence of these four conditions, one can readily see that it is possible to explain the emergence of the law as the core institution concerned with the management of conflict: not only were the violent alternative methods of settling disputes de-legitimated and indeed criminalised, but also court proceedings took a highly mannered, adversarial form.

Most of Elias' argument is either well-supported by historical evidence or at least plausibly argued. Where he seems to have been mistaken is in his conclusion as to its most important consequence of these developments which he specified as a dramatic reduction in the violence of everyday life. Elias was wrong about the high level of violence in feudal and especially 'simpler' societies, with respect to which he appears to have shared Hobbes' prejudiced view that 'life was nasty, brutish and short'(van Krieken, 1989). And he was also wrong about the low level of violence in contemporary societies, where he greatly underestimated the exponential rise in 'bureaucratic', war-like or war-related violence, which for Randell Collins (1974) has come perilously close to overcoming our 'resistance to killing', or that conception of human life that we owe to our most 'primitive' ancestors – those for whom human lives were so interdependent that none could be singled out even as a sacrificial object.

FOUCAULT ON THE INVENTION OF FREEDOM

A more general version of Elias's basic argument was later produced by Foucault. In order to grasp the nature of Foucault's contribution, it is necessary to embark on a brief excursus concerning his more general understandings of discourse and power. In the broadest terms, Foucault, like Elias, reworks themes extracted from Durkheim and Weber against a background that owes a lot to Marx's understanding of the nature of capitalism and the manner of its emergence from feudalism (Trombadori, 1991). More specifically, and to the present writer at least, Foucault's concept of discourse and his appreciation of its social significance appear to be akin to Durkheim's concept of collective representations. Also, Foucault's understanding of the nature of power seems to be similarly related to Weber's concept of power. What makes Foucault's reworking of these concepts particularly useful is: first, he rediscovers understandings of the areas of social life to which the concepts of discourse and power refer that had been lost as a consequence of sociology's transformation as it changed from being a largely European product to a transatlantic phenomenon; and second, he combines the concepts of discourse and power to produce a new understanding of the interrelationships between the social phenomena to which the concepts of discourse and power refer.

What had been lost as Durkheim's insistence on the importance of culture crossed the Atlantic was any sense of the complexity of the relations between the cultural and other dimensions of social life. In the hands of Talcott Parsons, for example, the cultural realm simply took the place of the economy in orthodox Marxism as the fundamental determinant of everything else. What had been lost as Weber's concept of power crossed the Atlantic was any sense of power as a way of summarising the outcome of what is in all significant instances a complex set of interactions. Instead, power came to be understood as some kind of substance or capability (Hindess, 1996). Weber defined power as follows: 'the chance of a man or a number of men to realise their own will in a communal action even against the resistance of others'. Thus Weber understood power to be a probabalistic phenomenon ('the chance of') that summarises the outcome of a complex set of factors and takes the form of a relationship which is never entirely one-way ('resistance' is part of the definition); that is, so far from power referring to a substance or capability of some kind, it provides a shorthand way of referring to a complex set of relations by referring to one of its outcomes, namely the triumph of one person's or group's will over another. Thus power is understood not as something that is distributed but as a product of a certain disposition of social relations. In apparently unknowingly rediscovering Weber's original concept of power, Foucault also recovered a Durkheimian appreciation of the complexity of the relations between the cultural and other dimensions of the social by seeing culture as always embedded in, and contributing to, the complex sets of relations that produce power differences.

In the present context, the most pertinent aspects of Foucault's rediscovered and new understandings of the conjoint existence of discourse and power are contained in his concepts of 'discursive formation' and 'governmentality'. The new analytical possibilities created by these concepts allow one, first, to grasp more adequately than before the complexity of the social developments involved in the empowering of the law; and second, to understand that one of the most significant consequences of the associated changes in the way in which states related to their subjects (governmentality) as they were made into citizens was an empowering of the the law. In the simplest sense, what Foucault refers to as discourses are the more or less formal sets of inter-linked concepts, whether in the form of religions, ideologies, sciences or whatever, that organise, order and constrain our thought. As such this is a very familiar even commonsensical idea. But what makes Foucault's deployment of it far from commonsensical is that he not only intuited that discourses do not achieve their effects by logic alone, but he also found a way to investigate the nature of the additional factors involved. This was the achievement of his earlier 'archae-ological' studies, which culminated in the *Archaeology of Knowledge* (1972) and the formal elaboration of the concept of the 'discursive formation' and its 'rules of formation'.

The questions that Foucault addresses with these concepts are: 1) How do discourses develop? 2) How do they come to be taken as comprising authoritative and therefore to some degree socially determinant statements about the nature of the world? His answer to these questions is that discourses develop and gain their determinative power as a consequence of the largely unwilled interaction between four elements: objects (the things they are about); modes of enunciation (the ways these things are spoken of); concepts (the intellectual constructs that are used to speak about them); and strategies (the ways in which these constructs are combined or thematised). What determines the nature and power effects of the interactions between these elements are their respective rules or, better, the social entities and processes that continuously determine their formation and re-formation.

In the case of objects these entities and processes, partially translated from Foucault's rather fearsome terminology, comprise: 1) the institutional sites wherein the objects of interest are problematised and so become socially visible – for example the Catholic confessional in the case of psychiatry, the marketplace in the case of economics, and the court in the case of law; 2) the appearance or presence of authorities of delimitation – experts and latterly professionals of all kinds – who possess the power to decide what is or is not an instance of the object of interest; and 3) the production or presence of a grid of specification produced by these experts which delimits the object of interest and distinguishes it from other objects – examples include general concepts such as the body, the economy, the polity, society, the law and human rights. Concerning enunciative modalities or ways of making statements, the entities and processes are: 1) the credentials of the qualified speakers; 2) the institutional sites from whence they speak; and 3) the modes of interrogation in which they engage (listening, questioning, or looking, for example). With respect to concepts, the entities and processes are: 1) their order and forms of succession or emergence and development; 2) their fields and forms of coexistence or the general methodologies that are used to determine their legitimacy as instances of knowledge; and 3) the procedures for intervention or the ways of working within the conceptual field as exemplified by rewriting, transcribing and translating. Finally, the entities and processes with regard to strategies are: 1) the identities, similarities, differences and combinations of such strategies; 2) the identification of thematic authorities, whether these are located within the field of discourse involved or external to it and are therefore authorities by analogy; and 3) the identification of the '*function* that the discourse under study must carry out *in a field of non-discursive practices*' (Foucault, 1972, p. 68, emphasis in original) such as the economic and political realms, and '*possible positions of desire in relation to discourse*' (ibid., emphasis in original). What, in sum, Foucault has provided us with is a means for thinking about and tracking the highly complex concatenations of discursive and non-discursive elements that produce such discourses as the law and international human rights.

When one thinks about Foucault's specification of these concepts, it quickly becomes clear that discourse is not simply a matter of words, ideas and logic but, as the ancient rhetoricians had also grasped, it also embodies various other occasions of, and processes for, the generation of power in that it is enunciated by people occupying particular positions in various institutional and more general social hierarchies. But what is power? How is it that discourses can affect people's behaviour? And more particularly, what is the nature of the power embedded in discourse? It seems to have quickly become obvious to Foucault that power was a far more diffuse and indeed widely diffused phenomenon than is commonly assumed. Thus it could not be simply some sort of substantive resource or capacity that could be monopolised by, for example, the state. Given his interest in the power of discourse, he decided to produce his own understanding of power in the course of the genealogical studies that culminated in *The History of Sexuality* (1979). In these studies his central substantive point is that the rise of penological and sexological discourses produced by 'experts' simultaneously contributed to the disciplining of the non-experts and excited the same non-experts to talk about issues they may never have discussed or even thought about before. This, in turn, created the possibility that expert authority might become divided and/or be challenged. His central theoretical point is the recovery of Weber's original understanding of power mentioned earlier:

'Power', insofar as it is permanent, repetitious, inert, and self-reproducing, is simply the over-all effect that emerges from all these mobilities, the concatenation that rests on each of them and seeks in turn to arrest their movement . . . power is not an institution, and not a structure; neither is it a strength we are endowed with; it is the name one that one attributes to a complex strategical situation in a particular society . . . Power is not something that is seized, or shared, something that one holds on to or allows to slip away; power is exercised from innumerable points, in the interplay of non-egalitarian and mobile relations.

(Foucault, 1979, pp. 93–4)

Towards the end of his life, Foucault turned his attention to the study of the techniques of power, to the study of what he called 'governmentality'. When comparing liberal states to the preceding feudal and absolutist states, he noticed that the mode of governance deployed by the liberal state was much less direct in that the citizenry were instructed in how to govern themselves and administratively supported in so doing. On Nikolas Rose's (1999) reading, these techniques represented a mode of 'governing at a distance' and, shockingly to some, their deployment produced and sustained a key element in the new system of liberal governance, namely 'freedom'. Thus instead of freedom being the natural condition of humanity before the existence of states, as it was for Locke, it is understood by Foucault to have been the more or less accidental creation of states as they gained knowledge of their populations and tried to work out how to govern them. That is, as the emergence of capitalism made it increasingly clear that labour was as important a source of national wealth as land, animals or natural resources, states sought knowledge of their populations through the gathering of stat(e)istics concerning such events as births, deaths and marriages, and such attributes as property ownership, occupation, education and health.

In this way, populations gradually gained individual identities as persons of a certain age and gender, members of particular families, inhabitants of particular towns and villages, and property-owners, craftsmen, or whatever. At the same time, on the basis of what in Continental Europe was termed the science of police, the state began providing help in developing individual skills, maintaining the population's health and sanity, and securing the safety of their persons and property, all of which produced additional sets of individuating records and possible knowledges. In sum, through a three-level process of observation, social support and state record-keeping, populations became both individuated and more or less capable of taking care of and managing themselves in a peaceable, productive and apparently self-governing way. Extending Foucault's argument somewhat, all this was secured by the state's gradual confirmation and autonomisation of an increasingly complex system of rights and modes of reasoning in terms of them allowing individuals to protect their stakes in the emerging order (for detailed specifications of a conception of the legal system and its mode of operation that are compatible with Foucault's approach, see: Durkheim, 1964, pp. 386–7; Woodiwiss, 1990a, pp. 112–20). Moreover, through the creation of the new social space latterly known as 'civil society' or the 'public sphere', an arena was created wherein the new citizenry, ostensibly protected by a right to freedom of expression, could argue over the best ways in which to organise and govern themselves in pursuit of whatever might be their chosen preferences. This, then, is a Foucaultian explanation of how the legal system came to represent a new simulacrum of a just social order.

CONCLUSION

For Renner and Pashukanis, rights became part of an emerging set of what eventually became known as capitalist social relations and were attached to individuals in order to protect the property required for production, the commodities produced and indeed the individuals involved from arbitrary depredations and detentions on the part of the feudal authorities. For Weber and Durkheim, no sooner did rights emerge than they began to take on a life of their own, not only because of the increasingly technical and rule-bound character of the process of attachment (Berman and Reid, 1996) but also because rights were often presented outside the courts in mythic terms that suggested that rights were supra-legal ethical constructs rather than simply profane legal constructs. Developing Elias' analysis, thanks to the state's gradual monopolisation of force and the power to levy taxes, rights became more and more effective as legal constructs but initially only so far as property owners were concerned. The mythic terms in which this achievement was explained and justified, however, not only legitimated the profane efforts on behalf of owners but also excited others to think that one day they too might have liberties. Thus, following Foucault, the law as an element of the state and rights as an instrument and mode of governmentality both gained a certain autonomy from external influences, such as those constitutive of class relations, and became conduits of power in their own right: the law as an expert knowledge that evolved its own methodological rules, above all the general principle that these rules should be applied consistently, and rights as the entities known to this knowledge. Thus the formulation of a right to property implied an individual identity and a certain freedom that were in theory available to all, although few of the formally free were initially in a position to make any use of this new status and the state also simultaneously maintained many restrictions on such freedom.

Thus, contra Locke, and to repeat, neither rights nor indeed freedom existed in either an historical or an analytical sense prior to power, but both were constituted by, and constitutive of, a new mode of social life – capitalism. However, the ideas of freedom and rights not only contributed to the production of social divisions and corporate identities but they also provided the language that enabled these divisions and identities to be discussed and contested. Thus rights came to be seen, much to Marx's annoyance (as he explained in his *Critique of the Gotha Programme*), not just as means of exercising power but also as prizes or objects of desire, so to speak: valuable prizes in that they can enlarge the sphere of freedom and bring the power of the state onto the winner's side; but limited prizes in that neither the value of autonomy nor that of reciprocity is necessarily antithetical to the continuation of the inequality that is a necessary prerequisite for, as well as a consequence of, the existence of capitalism. In sum, then, as the sociological understanding of the law and rights has developed, the result has been an increasing capacity to appreciate not only the social constructedness of rights as products of discursive formations, but also their independent significance as elements in the generation of power.

3

FROM RIGHTS TO LIBERTY IN ENGLAND AND THE UNITED STATES

As far as I know no one has yet written a Foucaultian account of the development of either English common law or, more particularly, the emergence of rights discourse within it. This is clearly not the occasion to attempt such a task, nor indeed do I have the necessary knowledge. However, in order to make my point about the specificity and complexity of the history of our present array of civil rights, I will now provide a sociological and lightly Foucaultian outline of how the emergence of the rights to own property, work and make contracts was thematised as the rise of liberty or freedom. Thus, to use the formal Foucaultian vocabulary just once, I will be looking how a particular array of 'concepts', namely certain rights, was produced, formed into a distinctive 'strategy' of governance by being thematised as instances of liberty, in the context of the rise of the new 'enunciative modality' represented by legal discourse, and against the background of the problematisation of the 'object' represented by the changing relations between the state and its subjects produced by the transition from feudalism to capitalism.

At least for England, and as Weber also concluded, a legal system centred on non-capitalist concepts of ownership – that is, feudal 'dominium' (see above, p. 23) and petty commodity production (see above, p. 18) – was initially more than 'good enough' to contribute to the development of, and secure, capitalist relations of production despite its far from perfect fit (for a parallel analysis of the criminal law, see D. Hay *et al.*, 1975). As regards feudal 'dominium', a weakening of, and ultimately breaks in, the tenurial chain of landholding were achieved without the chain being destroyed altogether. Nevertheless, and despite counter developments with reference to 'settlements', the effect of these changes to the tenurial chain was sufficient to enable a market in land to develop. Similarly, a loosening and even escape from many of the constraints intrinsic to feudal labour relations were achieved without the latter's total destruction. Nevertheless, and again despite the state's attempts to reimpose the constraints (e.g. the Statutes of Labourers of 1349, 1351 and 1388), these developments were sufficient to allow changes to the meaning of property to have consequences with reference to how the land or whatever was worked. More specifically they allowed the imposition of tighter methods of control within the new capitalist workplaces than were characteristic of the manor or the feudal workshop, and this despite the efforts of guilds, sometimes the state (e.g. through master–servant laws) and latterly combinations or trade unions to resist them.

Thus, acknowledging the varying and changing fortunes of those engaged in any or all of the struggles around these issues, and despite the temporal and geographical unevenness of developments with respect to each of them, feudal law gradually made room for simple commodity producers and capitalist entrepreneurs. The general trajectory of this adjustment was determined by the interplay between the defensive demands addressed to the courts by the lordly property holders and the assertive demands for support addressed to the courts by the newer property owners. Hence the latter, whether they were lords or former serfs, whether their ancestral tenures were free or unfree, either initially requested or demanded support that tended to be confined to the realm of their exchanges of either property or goods and seldom related to issues directly arising out of their relations with their employees. Hence also the shift in what might be called, at the risk of an accusation of teleology, the 'pre-history of contract' from the very specific early forms of tort actions ('debt', 'detinue', 'covenant' and 'account'), to the later (fourteenth to fifteenth century) more general actions ('trespass', 'trespass on the case', '*indebitatus assumpsit*') and doctrines ('consideration'), which eventually coalesced in Slade's Case (1602) and created the beginnings of a discourse just about recognisable as what today is called 'contract' (Baker, 1979).

The critical legal and political developments that led to the thematising of the overall meaning of all these complex but decidedly mundane developments with respect to property and contract as the culmination of a process of rediscovering a supposedly ancient freedom or liberty and therefore instances of a special type of rights were fourfold: the gradual development of the writ of *habeus corpus*, the publication of Sir Edward Coke's *Institutes of the Laws of England*, the 'Glorious Revolution'of 1688, and the publication of Sir William Blackstone's *Commentaries on the Laws of England*.

Between the fifteenth and eighteenth centuries, the writ of *habeus corpus* – the literal meaning of the latin phrase is 'have the body' – gradually developed as a means of ensuring the observance of what eventually became known as due process (that is, minimally, the laying of formal charges and the occurrence of a court hearing) in cases where people had ended up, or might end up, in prison (Baker, 1979, pp. 168–9). Initially developed to prevent lower level state functionaries from arbitrarily imprisoning people, *habeus corpus* eventually became a constraint on the arbitrary actions of the state as such. Between 1628 and 1644, and no doubt emboldened by the gestation and onset of the Civil War to tell the story of the law as a narrative of liberty, Sir Edward Coke published his very influential, four-volume *Institutes of the Laws of England*. Although these volumes largely consisted of commentary on discrete and specialised points of law, what made them widely influential were the elements of systematisation they provided. The most historically significant of these elements were the consistent use of the term 'rights' as opposed to 'wrongs' to specify the basic units of the law, and the outrageous way in which volume one (on tenures and property) is linked with volume two (on 'ancient and other statutes'). What Coke argued was that all the mundane property rights specified in the first volume had their 'roote', through due process and by implication, therefore, partly through habeas corpus, in Magna Carta which is discussed at the beginning of the second volume. For Coke, Magna Carta was 'the charter of liberty because it maketh freemen', who are 'entitled to property, job, liberty, customs, freedoms by . . . [their] "birth-right."'

What made the link outrageous were two things. First, Magna Carta had played no civil-libertarian role in either legal reasoning or the deciding of cases before the publication of the *Institutes*. Second, as Coke surely knew, although Magna Carta did indeed give certain rights to freemen, the freemen it referred to were not ordinary people but the Barons who had forced King John to sign. Thus the idea that Magna Carta is the source of English, let alone any other nation's, liberty is a myth. However, that this myth was so quickly accepted as fact confirms the operation of the powerful social forces that the classical sociological theorists were later to descry and Locke was, literally, to naturalise with his celebrated retrojection of individualism and private property back to the 'state of nature' some forty-six years later in his *Second Treatise on Civil Government* (1689). Not that Locke had any idea that he was participating in myth making. As far as he was concerned, and reasonably so since his argument was firmly based in the historical data available at the time, he was simply applying his god-given reason to imagine the history of his present. Hence the immense and indeed serene self-confidence of his text, as illustrated by this extract:

> To understand political power aright, and derive it from its original, we must consider what estate all men are naturally in, and that is, a state of perfect freedom to order their actions, and dispose of their possessions and persons as they think fit, within the bounds of the law of Nature, without asking leave or depending upon the will of any other man.
>
> (Locke, 1689, para. 4)

What is more, just a year before Locke's book was published, Parliament had passed *The Bill of Rights* that was the culmination of the Glorious Revolution of 1688, and in so doing had seemed to confirm the depth of the English commitment to liberty by extending it to the political realm. Not only did the *Bill* announce itself, using Coke's language, '(as their ancestors in like case have usually done) . . . [as] vindicating and asserting their *ancient rights and liberties*' (emphasis added), and require the crown to recognise the rights of its subjects in criminal law, but it also required regular elections, more frequent parliamentary sessions and freedom of parliamentary speech.

When the first treatises on constitutional law were written in the latter part of the nineteenth century, the *Bill* too was mythologised as a great milestone in the development of democracy. This was despite the fact that, like Coke in relation to the Magna Carta, the treatise writers knew full well that the rights contained within the *Bill* were not only limited to those with very substantial property holdings but there was also absolutely no idea in the minds of the Bill's authors or supporters that these rights should ever be extended to those with lesser or no property holdings. As will become clear in the following chapter, society had to change considerably and the excluded groups had to fight for another century or two (especially in the case of women) before they gained such rights.

In the light of the Foucaultian approach taken here, it is at least arguable that an even more important textual milestone than any of those mentioned earlier in terms of embedding the idea of liberty within the routines of English life was the publication almost a 100 years after the Glorious Revolution of the first widely available legal 'self-help guide'.

This was Blackstone's *Commentaries on the Laws of England*, and this, corroboratively, is how Blackstone introduced it:

> I think it an undeniable pofition, that a competent knowlege of the laws of that fociety, in which we live, is the proper accomplifhment of every gentleman and fcholar; an highly ufeful, I had almoft faid effential, part of liberal and polite education.

(Blackstone, 1765–9, p. 6)

And what gave the *Commentaries* their doctrinal significance for rights discourse was that it was premised on a confidently elaborated and highly sophisticated conception of the 'absolute rights of man':

> THE abfolute rights of man, confidered as a free agent, endowed with difcernment to know good from evil, and with power of choofing thofe meafures which appear to him to be moft defirable, are ufually fumed up on one general appellation, and denominated the natural liberty of mankind. This natural liberty confifts properly in a power of acting as one thinks fit, without any reftraint or control, unlefs by the law of nature: being a right inherent in a us by birth, and one of the gifts of God to man at his creation, when he endued him with the faculty of freewill. But every man, when he enters into fociety, gives, up a part of his natural liberty, as the price of fo valuable a purchafe; and, in confideration of receiving the advantages of mutual commerce, obliges himfelf to conform to thofe laws, which the community has thought proper to eftablifh. And this fpecies of legal obedience and conformity is infinitely more defirable, than that wild and favage liberty which is facrificed to obtain it. For no man, that confiders a moment, would wifh to retain the abfolute and uncontrolled power of doing whatever he pleafes; the confequence of which is, that every other man would alfo have the fame power ; and then there would be no fecurity to individuals in any of the enjoyments of life. Political therefore, or civil, liberty, which is that of a member of fociety, is no other than natural liberty fo far reftrained by human laws (and no farther) as is neceffary and expedient for the general advantage of the publick

(Blackstone, 1765–9, p. 122)

Clearly dependent though this passage may be on the extract given earlier (see above p. 35) from Locke's *Second Treatise,* it entirely neglects two significant points. First, the stress that, later in the same chapter, Locke placed on the centrality of reciprocity to governance in the state of nature.

Second, for Locke, the problem that the social contract solved was the corruption produced by too much property and power rather than any chaos associated with freedom:

> when ambition and luxury, in future ages, would retain and increase the power, without doing the business for which it was given, and aided by flattery, taught princes to have distinct and separate interests from their people, men found it necessary to examine more carefully the original and rights of government, and to find out ways to restrain the exorbitances and prevent the abuses of that power, which they having entrusted in another's hands, only for their own good, they found was made use of to hurt them.
>
> (Locke, 1689, para. 111)

Although neither Locke before him nor Kant after him shared Blackstone's extreme individualism but instead allowed a significant role to reciprocity in their conceptions of a just society, Blackstone turned out to be more prescient than either of the others. I say this because for most of those who would later claim to follow Locke and Kant, the concept of autonomy rather than the combination of autonomy and reciprocity rapidly came to represent the core value on which the whole rights ediface rested. In this way autonomy became the basis of what might be termed the major rights tradition, leaving the combination of autonomy and reciprocity to provide the basis for a minor tradition.

This said, the Blackstonian broadcasting of the major tradition and the protection against, and remedies for, many personal wrongs that it provided, at least in theory, as part of the complex discursive and institutional matrix that eventually became known as the 'rule of law', may well have contributed to England's relative social stability during the otherwise turbulent period that followed the publication of the *Commentaries*. Elsewhere, however, thanks to authors such as Tom Paine, and drawing on the 'communist' ideas associated with such precursors of the minor tradition as the Ranters and Diggers of the English Civil war period (Hill, 1973), the ideas associated with natural rights eventually helped to provoke authentic revolutions, notably in the American Colonies and France. Hence the defining and somewhat broader declarations of what we now call civil rights contained within the American *Declaration of Independence* (1776), the French *Declaration of the Rights of Man and Citizen* (1789), and the American *Bill of Rights* (1791) that comprises the first ten amendments to the Constitution. The American *Declaration* lists the inalienable rights as 'Life, Liberty and the pursuit of Happiness', but both later compendia of rights focus almost entirely on the securing of liberty since the state is clearly regarded as the principle source of any threats to life or happiness. Thus even in their most expansive formulations, civil rights were and indeed remain largely concerned to limit the consequences of political inequality between the state and the citizenry. Significantly, at the point in time when they were written and even today, especially in the United States, economic inequality was and is unchallenged because, as both compendia make explicit, property ownership represents the principal mode of securing one's life and pursuing happiness.

Because of its iconic status, outside France, as the defining statement of civil rights, I will quote the American Bill of Rights in full:

AMENDMENT I
Congress shall make no law respecting an establishment of religion, or prohibiting the free exercise thereof; or abridging the freedom of speech, or of the press; or the right of the people peaceably to assemble, and to petition the Government for a redress of grievances.

AMENDMENT II
A well regulated Militia, being necessary to the security of a free State, the right of the people to keep and bear Arms, shall not be infringed.

AMENDMENT III
No Soldier shall, in time of peace be quartered in any house, without the consent of the Owner, nor in time of war, but in a manner to be prescribed by law.

AMENDMENT IV
The right of the people to be secure in their persons, houses, papers, and effects, against unreasonable searches and seizures, shall not be violated, and no Warrants shall issue, but upon probable cause, supported by Oath or affirmation, and particularly describing the place to be searched, and the persons or things to be seized.

AMENDMENT V
No person shall be held to answer for a capital, or otherwise infamous crime, unless on a presentment or indictment of a Grand Jury, except in cases arising in the land or naval forces, or in the Militia, when in actual service in time of War or public danger; nor shall any person be subject for the same offence to be twice put in jeopardy of life or limb; nor shall be compelled in any criminal case to be a witness against

himself, nor be deprived of life, liberty, or property, without due process of law; nor shall private property be taken for public use, without just compensation.

AMENDMENT VI
In all criminal prosecutions, the accused shall enjoy the right to a speedy and public trial, by an impartial jury of the State and district wherein the crime shall have been committed, which district shall have been previously ascertained by law, and to be informed of the nature and cause of the accusation; to be confronted with the witnesses against him; to have compulsory process for obtaining witnesses in his favor, and to have the Assistance of Counsel for his defence.

AMENDMENT VII
In suits at common law, where the value in controversy shall exceed twenty dollars, the right of trial by jury shall be preserved, and no fact tried by a jury, shall be otherwise reexamined in any Court of the United States, than according to the rules of the common law.

AMENDMENT VIII
Excessive bail shall not be required, nor excessive fines imposed, nor cruel and unusual punishments inflicted.

AMENDMENT IX
The enumeration in the Constitution, of certain rights, shall not be construed to deny or disparage others retained by the people.

AMENDMENT X
The powers not delegated to the United States by the Constitution, nor prohibited by it to the States, are reserved to the States respectively, or to the people.

Apart from the UDHR, the American Bill of Rights, and especially the First Amendment, is today probably the single most widely known rights text in the world. What is far less widely known outside of academia is that, like England's 'ancient liberties' (Ewing and Gearty, 2000, ch.1), the Bill of Rights offered little or no effective legal as opposed to rhetorical protection to the ordinary citizenry for the first 150 years or so following its ratification (Foner, 1999). This was for four reasons: first, in 1833 the Supreme Court had ruled that the *Bill of Rights* only applied to the actions of the federal government (Hargreaves, 2002, p. 256; Schwartz, 1977, pp. 202 ff.); second, the separate state governments and their courts were much more socially important than the federal government and its courts; third, until the economic and social legislation of the 1930s, there was little in the way of legislation for the courts to review; and fourth, the Bill of Rights could not protect citizens against what turned out to be the actions of the major threat to their liberties, namely the courts and their championing of property rights. Thus Bill of Rights protections, despite their repetition in many state constitutions (MacCray-Pearson, 1993), only became widely available to American citizens in the 1960s thanks to the decisions of the Supreme Court during the tenure of Chief Justice Warren (see below, ch. 8).

CONCLUSION

In his now classic study, *Social Justice*, David Miller (1976) summarises the story that has just been told by outlining three sociologically distinct forms of social justice:

> In primitive societies a traditional network of close personal relationships produces a commitment to values such as generosity [i.e. reciprocity] rather than to any concept of social justice. In hierarchical societies of the feudal type the combination of firmly established social ranking and a degree of personal contact across ranks leads to a primary emphasis on justice as the protection of established rights and a secondary emphasis on justice as the relief of the needy [i.e. reciprocity]. In market societies the predominence of impersonal exchange relationships leads to a new interpretation of justice as the requital of desert.
>
> (Miller, 1976, p. 338)

He concludes his summary by outlining how the tensions between autonomy and reciprocity apparent in Kant were played out, at least in Europe, in the course of the next 100 or so years:

> the transformation of these societies brought about chiefly by the rise of corporate groups has changed the basis of desert and reintroduced the principle of need as a subsidiary criterion of justice. Finally within market societies various groups suffering from social dislocation have responded by establishing egalitarian communities embodying a 'deviant' conception of social justice as distribution according to need.
>
> (Ibid., p. 339)

It was from the vantage point created by the third of these conceptions of social justice, that the currently most sociologically influential reading, in Europe at least, of the relation between rights discourse and an emergent capitalism was produced, namely Thomas Marshall's 'Citizenship and Social Class' (1949). Marshall's stance is frankly teleological, and therefore to some degree he is aware of the partiality of his reading. Thus he prefaces his account of the three phases of the development of what he calls 'citizenship rights' – civil rights in the eighteenth century, political rights in the nineteenth century and social rights in the twentieth century – by referring to the 'modern drive towards social equality' as 'the latest phase of an evolution of citizenship which has been in continuous progress for some 250 years' (Marshall, 1949, p. 73). In his initial definition of civil rights Marshall stays close to the late eighteenth-century conception: 'the civil element is composed of the rights necessary to individual freedom – liberty of the person, freedom of speech, thought and faith, the rights to own property and to conclude valid contracts and the right to justice' (ibid., p. 74). Moreover, he immediately comments on this list that:

> [t]he last is of a different order from the others, because it is the right to defend and assert all one's rights on terms of equality with others and by due process of law. This shows that the institutions most directly associated with civil rights are the courts of justice.
>
> (Ibid.)

However, when Marshall turns to the discussion of the relevance of the eighteenth century to the world circa 1949, his emphasis is rather different to that of Blackstone *et al.*, even if their judicial decisions were partly responsible for what strikes Marshall: 'In the economic field the basic civil right is [not property and certainly not the freedom of speech, thought or religion] but the right to work, that is to say the right to follow the occupation of one's choice in the place of one's choice, subject only to the legitimate demands for preliminary training' (ibid., p. 76). Marshall agrees with Richard Henry Tawney that this development meant that at last 'all men were free' (ibid., p. 79) and therefore represented the '"the final triumph of the common law" in regions [the employment relation], from which it had been excluded for four centuries . . . henceforth, . . . "there is, nominally at least, one law for all men"' (ibid., p. 79). In this way, then, for Tawney and Marshall like Durkheim, the propertyless finally found a place in the legal simulacrum of an interdependent communal life bequeathed to western societies by Roman law, or so they may have thought.

In conclusion, the entry of 'contract' into the spheres of property and employment, as the culmination of the process whereby legal discourse as a whole was elaborated and restructured, was simultaneously the moment at which individual autonomy became predominant within legal discourse, a new basis for juridical consistency was made available, and the wider social significance of this new system became clear: the requirements of those that most often made demands upon the law, namely the owners of capital, would now take precedence over all other concerns. That said, it should not be forgotten that another very important means by which capitalist employment relations were secured was by the gradual democratisation of the state. Indeed the entry of contract into the spheres of property and employment, as well, therefore, as the restructuring of legal discourse, was only possible because of this democratisation and the legislation it made possible. In this way, the potential for a challenge to the legal privileging of capital was created, but it took much longer to become a reality than is commonly supposed.

4

THE COMPARATIVE SOCIOLOGY OF RIGHTS REGIMES

For Marshall, the nineteenth century was the century of political rights in Britain. So it was in that the franchise and the right to stand for election were gradually extended. The result was that in Britain, as in much of the rest of western Europe, most propertyless men over the age of twenty-one could vote and stand for election by the end of the century. So it was also in the United States, in that by the 1860s most propertyless, white men over the age of twenty-one could vote or stand for election. However, the granting of these political rights had very divergent consequences on different sides of the Atlantic. In most of western Europe broad-based labour movements developed, took an independent political stance and forced the gradual recognition of a wide range of social rights, including the need to support the poor financially if they were to be able to enjoy their civil rights. In the United States, by contrast and until the 1930s, the newly enfranchised voters, whether propertied or propertyless, supported the Republicans in the North, unless they were Irish, in which case they joined the 'solid', white South in supporting the Democrats. Another result of the greater significance of regional and ethnic rather than class differences in the United States was that when trade unions appeared they organised a narrow range of workers – in the main skilled, Northern, white and Protestant workers – into a non-partisan labour movement that had no independent political presense and little interest in a social rights agenda (Davis, 1986). Moreover, the nineteenth century was most definitely not the century of political rights for women, for African-Americans, for the inhabitants of western Europe's non-settler colonies, and for the populations of those non-western nations that had narrowly escaped colonisation, such as Russia, China and Japan.

SOCIOLOGY AND THE VARIATION IN RIGHTS DISCOURSES

There are, of course, huge sociological and other literatures concerned with the reasons for these national differences. In this chapter, however, I will provide accounts of only those contributions that take a comparative, macro-sociological approach and bear most directly on the central concern of the present study – rights discourses and their associated conceptions of social justice. As in the case of the relationship between the development of capitalism out of feudalism and the initial emergence of rights discourse in the West, there is a remarkable degree of agreement amongst sociologists as to the reasons for the subsequent variations in the ways in which such discourses developed, or did not, in different western and non-western societies. The first and undoubtedly the most influential sociologist to address this issue in a systematic and sustained way was Barrington Moore who sought to extend the insights of Marx and Weber in particular to the issue of variation in the structure and tenor of social life and their relation to rights regimes which, of course, was an issue of which the classical theorists were barely aware. The first of what turned out to be a trilogy of studies by Moore was *Social Origins of Dictatorship and Democracy: Lord and Peasant in the Making of the Modern World* (1966), in which he returned to the period studied by the classical theorists.

Following Denis Smith's (1983, pp. 20–1) concise distillation of Moore's argument, three aspects of feudal conditions appear to have been critical in setting a society off in the direction of either democracy, and therefore the embedding of civil and political rights, or dictatorship. First, there was the nature of the relationship between the landed aristocracy and the monarchy. Where a balance of some kind was achieved, as in England, rights emerged in order to specify this balance and provide a means for either its maintenance or its more or less peaceful development. Where one party dominated, as in Prussia, Japan and China, the emergence of rights was either greatly delayed or took a very qualified form. Second, there was the nature and extent of the commercialisation of agriculture. Where commercialisation took a capitalist form and was extensive, as in England, common cause around the advancement of their rights was made between rural and urban capitalists, who had little to fear from an utterly dependent and fragmented labour force, and democracy was the eventual, if entirely unintended, outcome. The same result also occurred where a successful revolution took place under either of two sets of circumstances: where, because of the incompleteness of the expropriation of peasant entitlements under feudalism, the peasantry and its urban allies proved capable of turning defence into offence, as in France; or where a 'free' peasantry forged an alliance with their capitalist neighbours or masters against a common enemy such as that represented by the slave system of the southern United States. By contrast, where commercialisation neither took a capitalist form nor was very extensive, as in Prussia, Japan and China, dictatorship resulted when eventually capitalism became predominant. Third, there was the relationship between the landed aristocracy and the emergent bourgeoisie. Where these groups became allies against the monarchy, as in England, and in particular where the aristocracy became economically capitalistic whilst the bourgeoisie adopted an aristocratic social outlook, mutual toleration and indeed intermarriage became possible with the result that non-violent, electoral competition eventually became the preferred mode of seeking control of the state, thus favouring democratisation. Where the aristocracy retained its predominance over the bourgeoisie, as in Prussia, or lost it as a result of a peasant uprising, as in Russia and China, dictatorship of one kind or another was the result.

In his next book, *Reflections on the Causes of Human Misery and on Certain Proposals to Eliminate Them* (1972), Moore moved on from the attempt to explain why some societies had proved to be more hospitable to civil and political rights than others to examine the perennial causes of misery that afflict people whatever political arrangements govern their lives. He begins by distinguishing four causes of misery – war, poverty, injustice and persecution for one's beliefs – and arguing that humans very slowly became less and less tolerant of these causes as they gained mastery over nature. Gradually, a question arose that can be put as follows: 'If one can protect oneself against some at least of nature's threats why should one not be able to protect oneself against other humans?' The difficulty, however, was that attempts to improve human behaviour proved to be one of the principal causes of human misery. Indeed, on the basis of his studies of the German and Russian revolutions, Moore came to regard the misery so caused as far more reprehensible than what might be called 'ordinary cruelty'. Thus, in the case of poverty and injustice, he embraces a kind of stoicism in that he seems to be saying that it is better to tolerate ordinary cruelty than risk something worse through pursuing utopian phantoms like complete equality or direct democracy. Significantly in the context of the present argument, his main proviso is that such ordinary cruelty is nevertheless only tolerable when it occurs within the context of relationships governed by the value of reciprocity with the result that the loyalty of inferiors is rewarded by care from superiors.

The development of a modern ethic of reciprocity is the main theme of the last of the books in Moore's trilogy, *Injustice: the Social Basis of Obedience and Revolt* (1978). Here he makes it clear that his stoicism is sociologically rather than ethically or even anthropologically grounded:

> [T]he point I am trying to make is that reciprocity, and social co-operation more generally, do not flow inexorably from some innate tendency in human nature. Earlier we have noticed that moral rules whose violation arouses an anger that seems almost instinctive are not necessarily due to frustration of innate human tendencies by unjust or oppressive social arrangements. Rather the rules are the consequence of human nature in a painfully constricted social situation; to put the matter a bit too cynically, the consequence of an effort to make the best of a bad situation with considerable anger against those persons whose apparent lack of self-control threatens to make the situation even worse . . . Whatever there is in the way of social co-operation or co-ordination (of which reciprocity is only one form) is under continual threat . . . Where co-operation exists, it has to be created and continually re-created. Specific and identifiable human beings have to perform this act of creation and recreation . . . that is true of even so impersonal a mechanism as the modern capitalist competitive market.
>
> (Moore, 1978, pp. 506–7)

Given this conclusion, it is strange that in the course of constructing his oeuvre as a whole Moore should have paid so much attention to what might be called extreme assaults on inequality and so little to the European Christian and Social-Democratic traditions and achievements, since the final two sentences in the quotation just given would seem to summarise the ethics of these parties rather well.

In any event, this is the gap that subsequent sociologists of social justice have sought to fill by focusing on the explanation of the differing levels of reciprocity embodied in the welfare regimes of western Europe and the United States. Reflecting the fact that a critical variable in explaining the different levels of reciprocity appears to have been the nature, strength and mode of organisation of the trade union movement, as a collective embodiment of Moore's 'specific and identifiable human beings', all of these studies have focused on the late nineteenth and early twentieth centuries. For John Stephens (1979), the condition of the labour movement was *the* critical variable – where the trade union movement was strong and centralised, the social rights that give a concrete form to reciprocity were more fully developed, and where the labour movement was neither strong nor centralised social rights were less, in the United States much less, fully developed. For Gosta Esping-Andersen (1990), class alliances and the particular character of the social reform plans pursued were equally important in determining the levels of reciprocity achieved – the deeper the alliance forged between the working and the middle classes the more developed and securely embedded the ethic of reciprocity. For Nicos Poulantzas (1974), Dietrich Rueschmeyer *et al.* (1992), and Michael Mann (1993), who all agree with Stephens and Esping Anderson that the interactions between economic, political, ideological and class forces were of critical importance, a wide variety of other factors, ranging from the international and transnational locations and fates of states to the correctness or otherwise of the political decisions made by the actors involved, were also significant in determining the varying degrees of reciprocity in different societies.

CONCLUSION

In the next two chapters, I will illustrate the utility of the analyses just outlined by deploying some at least of the same ideas in the course of an investigation of the difference that social-structural variation made to the development of rights discourse in what, from a western European perspective, are the outlier cases represented by the United States and Japan. This said, I will outline the social-structural particularities of each case in only the most pre-emptory manner and will instead spend most of my time specifying the conceptual legal consequences of these particularities (for more developed analyses of the interrelationships between social-structural particularities and legal developments in the United States and Japan, see Woodiwiss, 1990b, 1992). This is both because of space constraints and because, as in the previous chapter, I am more interested in augmenting the extant sociological analytic by providing a general illustration of the Foucaultian point that, because of the power relations embedded in them as well as those made possible by their governmentalist effects (see above, p. 30), legal developments in themselves can have a determinative, if highly variable, effect on the development of rights discourses. I will therefore conclude this chapter with a brief outline of how the law came to be considered a manipulable instrument of governance.

As the common law became more and more important in the regulation of social life, it became on object of interest in itself. In the early years of the nineteenth century, some thinkers like Edmund Burke took comfort from the disorganised character of the law on the grounds that this reflected the disorganised nature of ordinary life and so ensured both that the solutions it offered to any problems would be practical and that freedom would not be organised out of existence. Others, however, like Bentham, saw chaos and the danger of disorder where such as Burke saw practicality and freedom. To overcome the chaos, Bentham embraced the cause of codification. And in order to overcome the danger of disorder he entirely rejected even the Blackstonian version of natural rights, famously declaring it to be 'nonsense upon stilts'; 'upon stilts' because, not only were such rights intellectual phantoms ('nonsense') in that they had never been legislated for, but also because they were dangerous, anarchical phantoms in that they could be used to incite people to strike down that which actually had been legislated. Thus his code was based not on any natural rights, as in the case of the *Code Napoleon,* but on the self-invented utilitarian principle of 'the greatest happiness for the greatest number'. Memorable though Bentham's language on these issues may have been, there was one idea that, at least in the short and medium terms, proved to be most influential on, and indeed damaging to, the social inclusiveness of rights discourse. This was his underlying 'legal positivism' or the idea that what counted as law was only that which could be seen in the 'black letters' of the law, whether such letters were to be found in the decisions of judges or, as Bentham preferred, in acts of legislation:

A law may be defined as an assemblage of signs declarative of a volition conceived or adopted by the *sovereign* in a state, concerning the conduct to be observed in a certain *case* by a certain person or class of persons, who in the case in question are or are supposed to be subject to his power.

(Bentham, 1782, p. 1, emphasis in the original)

Or, as his friend John Austin put it :

The existence of law is one thing; its merit or demerit is another. Whether it be or be not is one enquiry; whether it be or be not conformable to an assumed standard, is a different enquiry. A law, which actually exists, is a law, though we happen to dislike it, or though it vary from the text, by which we regulate our approbation and disapprobation.

(Austin 1995: p. 157)

In a way that will be explained in Chapter 5, it was Legal Positivism, then, rather than utilitarianism, which eventually allowed the common law to escape the dependence on reasoning by analogy that Weber was so patronising about and indeed at about the same time as he was concluding that it could not be done.

This said, systematisation was only achieved in Britain and the United States some fifty or so years after Bentham had made his attempt. In the meantime, Legal Positivism had come to be understood as insisting that the content of any such systematisation should be derived not from legislation but from the decisions made, and reasoning deployed, in actual cases. Consequently, those fifty or so years had a profound effect on the substantive principles subsequently embedded in the law and therefore on the law's wider social significance. For this reason, then, Chapter 5 will provide a brief account of the development of property and contractual rights in the United States, where in the absence of much, if any, judicial consideration, let alone enforcement, of the First Amendment freedoms (Foner, 1999), such developments were the major direct determinant of the nature of rights discourse. In Chapter 6, I will examine what happened when already codified continental law was imported into the very different social-structural context instanced by Japan, before returning to the issue of the significance of legal systematisation for rights discourses more generally.

5

FROM LIBERTY TO THE 'RULE OF (PROPERTY) LAW' IN THE UNITED STATES

As indicated in the previous chapter, one immediate cause of what ultimately proved to be the United States' outlier status with respect to rights discourse was its lack of a European-style labour movement prepared to push for the recognition of social rights. According to the pertinent literatures, and within the context of the social dynamics identified by Moore (see above, p. 45), the social-structural features responsible for this lack range from the absence of a feudal past, through the unusual diversity of its economic structure (capitalism in the North, slavery in the South and simple commodity production everywhere but especially in the West), its federal political system, and the early achievement of the universal white male franchise, to the highly diverse and geographically mobile nature of its largely immigrant labour force. However, a result of all of these particularities that was as significant an immediate cause of the United States' rights exceptionalism as the nature of the labour movement, was the fact that judge-made law played a much larger role in the determination of rights discourse than was the case in any western European country including Britain.

The first point to be made about the Republic's legal history is that the Revolution temporarily fractured the connection between law and the state that is essential to the achievement of successful disciplinary effects, given the intrinsically intermittent character of legal intervention. Moreover, the law that, somewhat fragilely, remained in force after the Revolution had severed it from the British state was the relatively unsystematic and still quite parochial common law of England. Had the inherited law been formalised as a code, it might have been possible to Americanise it more easily by, for example, ensuring that it was compatible with the *Bill of Rights*; and certainly such a process would have silenced the criticisms of those who equated the law as such with English law, and so claimed that it was un-American and unnecessary, despite the prominence of the Supreme Court in the Constitution. However, the inherited law was not formalised as a code and its antebellum (pre-Civil War) history was therefore marked by a struggle on the part of the leading jurists both to maintain continuity with British law in the form of lines of precedent and 'rules of law', and to make the laws themselves appropriate to, and legitimate under, post-revolutionary conditions.

Many commentators have been puzzled by the fact that American legal personnel, both lawyers and judges, proved to be in the main so extremely favourable to the holders of property rights. Much of the mystery disappears, however, when one remembers, despite the pretensions of many academic jurists, if not practising lawyers, that the private law, wherein rights discourse originated, developed as a response to client demands. Thus it developed, and still today develops, through the preparation of briefs which try to match the often somewhat ambiguous statements found in constitutions, statutes and earlier judgements with the desires of clients, of whom by far the largest number were and remain businessmen. Sidney Fine has concisely summarised the process whereby the sacred and the profane in the law were and are linked:

> Inasmuch as there has been a constant interaction between book, bar and bench, it is essential to take into consideration in this connection not only the views of judges but also those of lawyers and of the writers of legal textbooks. Legal textbooks provide convenient ideas and groupings of precedents for lawyers and judges to sample, and judges often find in lawyers' briefs arguments on which to base their opinions.
>
> (1964, p. 127)

Benjamin Twiss in his *Lawyers and the Constitution* (1962) and Clyde Jacobs in his *Law Writers and the Courts* (1954) have between them comprehensively and conclusively demonstrated the commitment of bar and books respectively to the property-centred ideas of laissez-faire liberalism (for an outline and critique of recent attempts to revise their conclusions see

Cachan, 2002). Similarly, many writers have commented upon the high number of ex-corporation lawyers and specifically railroad lawyers (among them Strong, Bradley, Waite, Shiras and Jackson) as well as the veritable philosophers of laissez-faire such as Field and Brewer to be found in the Supreme Court during the nineteenth century (Friedman and Israel, 1969). Thus, it would not be especially interesting to cite chapter and verse here in order to prove the overwhelming personal commitment to the sanctity of private property of those occupying important positions within the legal system. What is interesting, however, is the way in which such men, unconsciously at first, were able to make property rights central to American legal discourse as that discourse took a systematised form.

PROPERTY AND THE CHALLENGE TO STATE POWER

As was indicated in the previous chapter, a critical legal aspect of the transition from feudalism to capitalism was the strengthening of private property rights vis-à-vis the state. By the eighteenth century, the concept of private property had become what Morton Horwitz has called 'absolute', in that, for example, ownership of land 'conferred on an owner the power to prevent any use of his neighbour's land that conflicted with his own private enjoyment' (Horwitz, 1977, p. 31). This is the conception of property that allowed, as a consequence of the state's default amongst other things, the transfer of the rights to regulate labour from the state to the employer. As, however, the pace of economic development quickened in the early years of the nineteenth century, it became apparent that this form of property right was actually quite restrictive. It allowed the constriction of the rights of the more enterprising landowners, who very often sought to use their land for purposes that might interfere with their neighbours' 'quiet enjoyment'.

According to Horwitz, the history of property rights in nineteenth-century America may be divided into three stages, which he summarises in the following passage:

> In the first stage that continued until roughly 1825, the dominant theme was expressed by the maxim *sic utere*. Dominion over land was defined primarily as the right to prevent others from using their property in an injurious manner, regardless of the social utility of a particular course of conduct. This system began to break down in the second quarter of the nineteenth century as it became clear not only that common law doctrines led to anticompetitive results but that the burdens on economic growth under such a system might prove overwhelming.

Through limitations imposed on the scope of the nuisance doctrine, the emergence of the negligence principle, and the riparian doctrine of reasonable use, courts began to strike a balance between competing land uses, freeing many economically desirable but injurious activities from legal liability if they were exercised with due care. Thus, in a second stage, which crystalized by the middle of the nineteenth century, property law had come largely to be based on a set of reciprocal rights and duties whose enforcement required courts to perform the social engineering function of balancing the utility of economically productive activity against the harm that would accrue.

In the two decades before the Civil War, however, one detects an increasing tendency by judges to apply the balancing test in such a way as to presume that any productive activity was reasonable regardless of the harm that resulted. And out of this intellectual climate, a third stage began to emerge, which self-confidently announced that there were no legal restraints at all on certain kinds of injurious activities. In a number of new and economically important areas, courts began to hold that there were no reciprocal duties between property owners; that courts would not even attempt to strike a balance between the harm and the utility of particular courses of conduct. While this trend only reached its culmination after the Civil War, its roots were deep in an antebellum change in the conception of property. Dominion over land began to be regarded as an absolute right to engage in any conduct on one's property regardless of its economic value. Judges began to withdraw to some extent from their role of regulating the type and degree of economic activity that could be undertaken. And the mercantilist character of American property law was diluted by an emerging laissez-faire ideology.

(Horwitz, 1977, p. 102)

Thus, while the absolute conception of property right had allowed state charters and monopolies (Hartz, 1968) to resist legal challenges, it was the 'reasonable use' concept that undermined these charters and monopolies and, for example but as an unintended consequence, enhanced capital's capacity to discipline its labour force without fear of outside interference (see also, Horwitz, 1977, pp. 130–2).

In sum, the rights of private property were initially residual in that, as an inherited effect of English feudal law, they comprised what was left after the states had asserted their claims, especially through their power to grant monopolies to certain favoured property owners. Thus before the Civil War it was still possible for the states to determine how the newly independent concept of property should be articulated with other discursive elements such as labour, as, for example, in the case of the ten-hour laws passed by several state legislatures in the 1840's (see also, Novak, 1993). After the Civil War, this relationship was reversed and property rights became generative in that, to a far greater degree than in England, they dominated legal discourse in the economic sphere and set limits to the powers of the states, especially the federal state, and trumped all other rights.

CONTRACT: VISIONS AND DISAPPOINTMENTS

As Roger Cotterill (1981, p. 65) has stressed, contract had its origins in the feudal oath of fealty made by a tenant to his lord. The crucial difference between the feudal oath and the modern contract lies in the fact that the former, which was gradually formalised as a written 'contract', was in no way a promise made and accepted by legal equals as the concept of contract later came to require. Thus, contract was not itself intrinsically egalitarian and the equalisation of contractual relations had to be fought for politically and ideologically in each of the spheres within which it entered legal discourse. The history of the emergence of the concept of contract is, then, the history of various struggles for 'freedom of contract', where the freedom involved always requires release from obligations arising from relationships other than those set up by the contract itself, whether one is talking about property sales, employment relations, or marriages. This, to use Sir Henry Maine's famous phrase, is the history of the transition from 'status to contract'.

Over the same period that the concept of property was gaining its independence from the powers of the states so too was that of contract, which in the same movement also became independent of the concept of property, as will be shown below. In the legal discourse of feudalism, the fulfilment of any economic contractual obligation was dependent upon the fairness of the proposed exchange. Every commodity had its 'just price', which was established by local custom and enforced by the local magistrates. If a particular exchange departed from these prices, that exchange could be refused by the wronged party. As markets grew beyond their initially very local confines and money became the common medium of exchange, this conception of contractual obligation became increasingly inappropriate. Horwitz gives the reasons for this in the following passage:

> In a market, goods came to be thought of as fungible; the function of
> contracts correspondingly shifted from that of simply transferring title

to a specific item to that of ensuring an expected return. Executory contracts, rare during the eighteenth century, became important as instruments for 'futures' agreements; formerly, the economic system had rested on immediate sale and delivery of specific property. And most important, in a society in which value came to be regarded as entirely subjective and in which the only basis for assigning value was the concurrence of arbitrary individual desire, principles of substantive justice were inevitably seen as entailing an 'arbitrary and uncertain' standard of value. Substantive justice, according to the earlier view, existed in order to prevent men from using the legal system in order to exploit each other. But where things have no 'intrinsic value', there can be no substantive measure of exploitation and the parties are, by definition, equal. Modern contract law was thus born staunchly proclaiming that all men are equal because all measures of inequality are illusory.

(Horwitz, 1977, p. 161)

In response to these developments, the doctrine of the 'just price' was gradually and unevenly displaced by 'the will theory of contract' that so excited Durkheim, and whereby the mutual exchange of promises alone came to be understood as creating the contractual obligation. With this change in the concept of contract, its independence from that of property was obtained, since any breach thenceforth entitled the injured party not to 'specific performance' or delivery of the commodity in question, but to damages for the breach itself. Nevertheless, although according to the will theory the parties to a contract are equal in their mutual desire for the exchange and their status before the courts, this equality was not necessarily extended and reproduced by the decisions of the courts. Once a contract was regarded as the product of two or more wills, custom and practice did not become completely irrelevant since they entered an agreement as implied terms even if they were not expressly part of it. In one area, in particular, this distinction between express and implied terms was used to the systematic disadvantage of one of the parties:

The most important class of cases to which this distinction applied was labor contracts in which the employee had agreed to work for a period of time – often a year – for wages that he would receive at the end of his term. If he left his employment before the end of the term, jurists reasoned, the employee could receive nothing for the labor he had already expended. The contract, they maintained, was an 'entire' one, and therefore it could not be conceived of as a series of smaller agreements. Since the breach of any part was therefore a breach of the whole, there was no basis for allowing the employee to recover 'on the contract'. Finally, citing the new orthodoxy proclaimed by the treatise writers, judges were led to pronounce the inevitable result: where there was an express agreement between the parties, it would be an act of usurpation to 'rewrite' the contract and allow the employee to recover in quantum meruit for the 'reasonable' value of his labor.

(Horwitz, 1977, p. 186)

Despite the disadvantageous consequences of these changes in the concept of contract for this particular group of workers, overall and at least for a while they represented an advance, since they allowed the law to recognise the difference between journeymen who worked for a simple commodity-producing master and those who worked as wage-labourers for a capitalist. Within the employment relation, the terms upon which the ownership of property engendered, to use Renner's term, an 'order of goods' were changed as this ceased to be a prerogative of the master and became the object of a contract and therefore possible negotiation between the wage-labourer and the employer. Thus, if the development of legal discourse in the antebellum period saw the growing independence of the concept of the property, it also saw the increasing independence of contract. And, as property became independent of the states' powers, so contract became independent of custom and thereby allowed property to be articulated directly with labour. Together, these developments had the effect, on the one hand, of freeing the employment relation from direct regulation by the state and, on the other, of allowing it to be governed by individual agreements between employers and employees. This, then, is how developments in contract law made possible Durkheim's vision of a society based purely on voluntary agreements.

THE PRIVILEGING OF PROPERTY

Unfortunately for Durkheim's vision, the ongoing development of the concept of property allowed the general reintroduction of restrictions on labour's freedom of contract and preferred modes of contract enforcement; that is, the rights of property were broadened so that labour's actions in picketing, striking or boycotting were very often found to be in violation of the rights of property, to be injurious of them. By the early years of the twentieth century, property had ceased to be an indivisible unity and what Grey (1980) calls 'thing-ownership' or what John R. Commons (Commons, 1924) called 'corporeal', and had become instead 'a bundle of rights' some of which referred to its 'intangible' as well as its 'corporeal' dimension (see also, Hohfeld, 1919; and Horwitz, 1992, ch. 5). Put very simply, this transformation involved the addition to the fundamental ownership rights in productive things of certain rights allowing the value-creating uses to which the property was put to be regarded as intrinsic to it, and therefore as also deserving the protection of the law. As Commons put it, using the language of political economy, what the law came to protect was not simply the 'use-value' but also the 'exchange-value' of property.

In the course of the Supreme Court's *Slaughter House* cases of 1872 and 1884, which concerned the rights of the state of Louisiana to grant a monopoly to particular slaughter house owners in New Orleans and then to change the grantees, the view that exchange-value should also be protected appeared first in a dissent and then in a joined majority decision (Commons *et al.*, 1924, ch. 2). Even in the 1884 case, however, the only authority cited in support of the new definition of property was Locke's student, Adam Smith, whom Justice Field quoted as follows: 'The property which every man has in his own labour, as it is the original foundation of all other property, so it is the most sacred and inviolable' (Commons *et al.*, 1924, p. 14). Despite the fact that this was still a minority definition of property amongst the Justices of the Supreme Court, it nevertheless crept into the purportedly constitutional definitions given in state and federal courts, gradually gaining acceptance until it finally became the majority definition in the Supreme Court itself on the occasion of the *Minnesota Rate Case* of 1890 (Commons *et al.*, 1924, pp. 14–17). In Paul's (1960, p. 106) words: 'Property had . . . thus become the equivalent of the continued profitableness of the employer's business.'

All of this occurred despite the fact that the broadening of the substantive rights granted to property owners actually called into question the applicability of Locke and Smith's definition. As Commons pointed out, the rights intrinsic to property as use-value were those that protected production as such, whereas those intrinsic to exchange-value, to 'continued profitableness', were those that protected what he called the 'bargaining power' of owners in relation to both employees and customers:

> Bargaining power is the wilful restriction of supply in proportion to demand in order to maintain or enlarge the value of business assets; but producing power is the willing increase of supply in order to enlarge the wealth of nations.
>
> Hence the transition in the meaning of property from the use-value to the exchange-value of things, and therefore from the producing power that increases use-values to the bargaining power that increases

> exchange-values, is more than a transition – it is a reversal. The reversal
> was not at first important when business was small and weak – it
> becomes important when Capitalism rules the world.
>
> (Commons *et al.*, 1924, p. 20)

Thus, in Commons' view, the enlarged bundle of rights granted to property
owners did not simply allow property owners to act contrary to the
expectations that for Locke and Smith legitimated their initial rights, but
also thereby undermined their entitlement to freedom to exercise those
rights without government interference. If property owners no longer
necessarily increased the 'wealth of nations', what entitlement did they
have to special protection by the law?

Although Commons' scepticism was to become widely shared in the
1930s, few shared it in the last decade of the nineteenth century. Instead,
because of the transformation that has just been sketched, property became
for a time the virtually unqualified core element of legal discourse. Indeed
it had become generative in that, as it changed, so other concepts tended
to change to accommodate it, at least if they were discursively relevant.
The rights of which it was composed required the redefinition of other
rights, and the reordering of legal discourse, and, in many instances, these
changes were accomplished. In particular, the power of the state, which
Commons looked to as a source of a possible counter-discourse to that
of property, had not simply been displaced by property from its core position, but had also become property's principal support by virtue of the
transformation of the meaning of the 'due process' clause contained in
the Fourteenth Amendment to the Constitution (Woodiwiss, 1990b,
pp. 99–108). Remarkably, but again because of the generative power of
property, an amendment that had been designed to prevent the return
of slavery was transformed into one that also prevented the state from
limiting the freedom of property holders in almost any way and despite
the radically changed nature of such holders – a change which again
challenged the applicability of Locke and Smith's crucial argument.

This latter change was that represented by the dramatically transformed
economic and legal nature of the most powerful producers of exchange-
value consequent on the emergence of ever larger and increasingly
oligopolistic corporations that were granted 'legal personality' (Friedman
1973, ch. 8; Horwitz, 1992, ch. 3). The significance of this was again well
put by Commons:

> The corporate franchise prolongs the life of the association beyond the
> expectations of any individual. It binds a minority, without their consent,

if necessary, to act as a unit with the majority. It relieves individuals of responsibility beyond a certain limit, and limits the total responsibility to the amount of property owned by the corporation. Immortality, self-government, and limited liability are thus the sovereign powers and immunities granted to persons, collectively and individually, in order that a single will may act through agents in dealing with the rest of the world. Thus, the unit of property, a going business, is separated from individuals and is given an independent existence, an industrial government of its own, and a capacity of growth unknown to the natural person.

(Commons *et al.*, 1924, pp. 292–3)

Given that corporations were rapidly becoming the most powerful producers of exchange-value and that the labour of their owners made little or, in the case of shareholders, no contribution to this, it is difficult to see what pertinence Smith's argument had to the protection of their property rights. Indeed, a strict interpretation of what had become the constitutional definition of property should in fact have excluded them from the associated protections. In sum, and despite the problems that the broadening of substantive property rights and the changing nature of the subject bearing these rights may have appeared to cause for the continuing validity of Smith's enabling argument, the definition of property changed so that it was understood that an 'irreparable injury' could be inflicted in the course of a trade dispute in the sense that an opportunity to make profit was lost as a consequence. This would have nullified labour's First Amendment rights in the economic sphere, had labour been enjoying any.

THE 'RULE OF LAW' AS A GOVERNMENTALITY

The developments outlined above provided the substantive content for both a systematised and supposedly objective legal discourse and what became known as the 'rule of law'. The key figure as regards systematisation was Christopher Columbus Langdell, who was the Dean of Harvard Law School for much of the last quarter of the nineteenth century. The key figure as regards the formalisation of the rule of law was, as in England, Alfred Venn Dicey.

Because Langdell and the other 'formalists' were interested in establishing a scientific jurisprudence, and because they identified the scientific method with empiricism, they insisted that the principles they enunciated arose inductively out of the cases classified as relevant. Hence, their substitution of books of cases for interpretive treatises in their teaching after the American Civil War. Hence, also, the rise of law schools and departments in universities, as well as of other providers of training and discipline like bar associations (Chase, 1982; Nelson, 1982; Gilmore, 1977; Stevens, 1983; Sugarman, 1986). However, the critical question faced by all empiricists may also be posed to the Legal Formalists: how can one classify the relevant cases in advance of possession of the concept from whence the rules for their recognition may be derived? The answer is that one cannot, and, moreover, the Langdellians, like most creative empiricists in other disciplines, did not try. Instead, the Langdellians, like their English counterparts, started from the concepts found in the treatises of Blackstone and such as his American successors, James Kent and Joseph Storey, and rationalistically supported their reformulations, elaborations and 'systematisations' by reference to carefully selected cases. This is how Grant Gilmore – a more rigourously empiricist critic of the 'formalists' – makes the point:

> Langdell has pointed out that the law library was our laboratory and that the printed case reports were our experimental materials. It followed, therefore, that we were to study the cases and that, in our teaching, case-books were to replace treatises. It was, however, no part of Langdell's scheme that we were to study all the cases:
>
> > (T)he cases which are useful and necessary for (the purpose of mastering legal principles or doctrines) bear an exceedingly small proportion to all that have been reported. The vast majority are useless, worse than useless, for any purpose of systematic study (Langdell, 1881; as quoted in Sutherland, 1967, p. 174).
>
> Thus the vast majority of all reported cases, past and present are worse than useless and should be disregarded. The function of the legal scholar, whether he is writing a treatise or compiling a case-book, is to winnow out from the chaff those very few cases which have ever been correctly decided and which, if we follow them, will lead us to the truth. That is to say, the doctrine – the one true rule of law – does not in any sense emerge from the study of real cases decided in the real world. The doctrine tests the cases, not the other way around.
>
> (Gilmore, 1977, p. 4)

In Chapter 2, it was suggested that, as long as the idea of a systematised legal discourse remained a mere aspiration, interested parties were free to project whatever vision of the just community they wished upon it, as indeed Bentham's Utilitarian effort at codification illustrates (see also, Greenberg, 2001, for accounts of some minor-tradition readings of the 'ancient constitution' invoked by Coke). Ironically, once such a system-atised discourse was in fact achieved it was considered to be not only distinct from the rights upon which it rested, but also, because of its 'scientific' nature, to be superior to them in value, especially for those unfortunate peoples who had not been as lucky as England and, by extension, the United States since they had not been blessed with a legacy of 'ancient liberties'. Hence the British and American insistence on the inclusion of extraterritorial jurisdiction clauses, which prohibited the local trial of their citizens, in the 'unequal treaties' forced on states that could be bullied though not conquered, such as Japan, China and Korea. Thus, and notwithstanding the efforts of John Stuart Mill (1859) on behalf of a more expansive conception of liberty, by the end of the nineteenth century what was celebrated in, and proudly exported by, Europe and the United States was not a bill of rights but the 'rule of law', not an array of freedoms but a very substantial piece of governmental machinery, not a set of potentialities but a system for constraining them as has been made very clear in many excellent studies of colonial law (Darian-Smith and Fitzpatrick, 1999; Fitzpatrick, 2001; Hooker, 1978).

Ironically, such constraint also limited the possibilities for social development and the enhancement of social reciprocity in those countries that had benefited most from the 'blessings of liberty'. This was because, as has been made clear, the legal content of the rule of law was not sub-stantively neutral at all since property rights rather than any others provided its core. Nowhere is the domestically constraining character of the rule of law more clearly apparent than in the work of the originator of the concept, Dicey, whose textbook, *Introduction to the Study of the Law of the Constitution,* was first published in 1885:

> The rule of law, as described in this treatise, remains to this day a distinctive characteristic of the English constitution. In England no man can be made to suffer punishment or to pay damages for any conduct not definitely forbidden by law; every man's legal rights or liabilities are almost invariably determined by the ordinary Courts of the realm, and *each man's individual rights are far less the result of our constitution than the basis on which that constitution is founded* . . .
>
> It means, again, equality before the law, or the equal subjection of all classes to the ordinary law of the land administered by the ordinary Law Courts; the 'rule of law' in this sense excludes the idea of any exemption of officials or others from the duty of obedience to the law which governs

other citizens or from the jurisdiction of the ordinary tribunals (emphasis added).

The constraint arose because the 'rights . . . on which that constitution is founded', were rigourously limited to the supposedly ancient ones to 'personal freedom; the right to freedom of discussion; the right of public meeting', whose principal purpose, as he subsequently insisted increasingly strongly as his book went through successive editions, was keeping 'secure or sacred' a deeper layer of rights, namely 'private rights' or 'the important rights of individuals . . . [that is,] property or . . . the contracts of private persons'. Thus he was untroubled by the fact that many laws severely limited the 'ancient rights' of the propertyless (Ewing and Gearty, 2000, ch.1). In other words, the law's constraining of the possibilities for social development arose because the economic system based on the supposedly most ancient rights of property and contract, capitalism, had displaced the person as the sacred grounding of the law:

> The principles that guide us, in public and in private, as they are not of our devising, but moulded into the nature and the essence of things, will endure with the sun and moon – long, very long after Whig and Tory, Stuart and Brunswick [suffragist, suffragette, and anti-suffragist], and all such miserable bubbles and playthings of the hour, are vanished from existence and memory.

Moreover, Dicey was nothing if not consistent in that he frankly acknowledged that following such principles meant accepting all other inequalities. Hence his bitter opposition to trade union use of the freedoms of speech and association – 'the triumph of legalised wrongdoing' – and the idea of enfranchising women, which he argued should be rejected because:

> [i]t treats as insignificant for most purposes that difference of sex which, after all, disguise the matter as you will, is one of the most fundamental and far-reaching differences which can distinguish one body of human beings from another.

Thus, from the moment the rule of law was 'discovered', any effort to assert any rights other than those considered ancient and/or private or to extend them to ordinary men and women, had to overcome an enormous disadvantage in that it appeared to challenge the rule of law and also therefore both the authority of science and, allegedly, the very idea of a just community. In sum, at the same moment as Weber's disparaging remarks about common law reasoning were proved to be unjustified, so Durkheim's hopes for the doctrine of contract and therefore for a society created by voluntary agreements, were already impossible before he voiced them – and both as a consequence of the same development, namely the achievement of the 'rule of (property) law'.

6

JAPAN, THE RULE OF LAW AND THE ABSENCE OF LIBERTY

I now wish to turn to a case where, in contrast to the United States, the summary difference in the nature of rights discourse as compared to western Europe is most often understood as an insufficiency, rather than a surfeit, of individualism, namely Japan. According to the pertinent literatures, most of the social-structural particularities of nineteenth-century Japan which, as a consequence of the dynamics specified by Moore (see above, p. 45), accounted for this insufficiency may be derived from the especially elaborate nature of the feudal system constructed under the Tokugawa Shogunate during the country's 250 years of seclusion from the rest of the world. Thus, even after the Meiji Restoration of 1868 which ended the seclusion as well as the feudal system, the economy was not in any sense straightforwardly capitalist, the state was in no way representative and the culture was not at all individualistic. The latter was instead strongly patriarchalist[1] in that the norms of the traditional family, wherein loyalty or filial piety is exchanged for paternal benevolence, summarised the dominant values. Also, there was no labour movement of any consequence and the judiciary had neither independence nor access to a unified and coherent body of independently generated law that had to be universalistically applied to both the citizenry and the state (Henderson, 1968b, pp. 415 ff.).

In the same way that Anglo-American law had feudal roots so too did Japanese law. However, Tokugawa law remained in force until the activation of the new Codes in the 1890s and indeed continued to mark 'modern' Japanese law until well into the twentieth century. The Tokugawa system has been described in great detail by Daniel Fenno Henderson in his monumental work *Conciliation and Japanese Law* (1977), Elsewhere Henderson has outlined the system in the following terms:

> The entirety of Tokugawa legal phenomena was a highly complex accumulation of imperial symbolism; a federalistic, doubledecked, feudal order; an elaborate status hierarchy of great constitutional import resting solidly on the rice tax; a base of rural villages regulated intra-murally by diverse customary laws covering the whole range of private transactions; and a Confucianistic family system – all made plausible by the isolation policy. As a whole these features may be regarded as a constitution in the English sense, articulated by some key, piecemeal, positive law decrees (e.g. the *buke-shohatto* and isolation decrees), customary practices, and precedents, all rationalised by orthodox Tokugawa Confucianistic philosophy (*shushigaku*). Clearly considerable positive law was generated by the shogunate (and *daimyo* [lords]), . . . it is necessary first to understand the shogunate's own thinking about law itself. Essentially, it was a natural law approach (*ri* as formulated in *shushigaku*). The static legal order was regarded as both natural and just, and positive law decrees were largely declaratory of these laws of nature. Even in the positive law there was little concept of made-law, for the efficacy of human endeavor to shape its environment was at the time low, and the concepts of law reflected that fact.
>
> (Henderson, 1968b, pp. 393–4)

This very definitely feudalistic legal system pivoted around the main-tenance of imperial and lordly landholding through the reinforcement of 'The Five Relationships' – sovereign/subject, husband/wife, parents/children, brothers/sisters, and friendship – central to the patriarchalist neo-Confucianism that had become the dominant discourse of rule in the mid-seventeenth century. Nevertheless, by the end of the eighteenth century, this legal system was made/able to find room for the existence of simple commodity and even capitalist production, as it did in England. This it did, despite or because of the existence of legislation to the contrary, through a device known as *dappo koi*. This was a legal fiction whereby it appeared that land had been transferred in payment of a debt rather than on payment of a price (Henderson, 1974, pp. 58–9). In this way a surrogate right to the ownership of private property was established even before the Restoration.

Most prominent amongst the feudal legal ideas that were continued after the Restoration and indeed later repeated in the 1890 Constitution and the new legal Codes were those that related to the position of the *tenno* or emperor and to family relations (that is, to those most pertinent to the direct maintenance of Confucian patriarchalism and its component ideas of 'loyalty' and 'filial piety' at the macro and micro levels of social life respectively). The effects of these continuations were not confined, however, to those areas to which they most directly referred but gave a distinctive cast to legal discourse as a whole. Both the repetition of these ideas and of this result were linked through relations of mutual entailment to the continuation of the general form of the Tokugawa law/society relation in post-Restoration society: where there is patriarchalist right and a means of successfully enforcing it, there is certainly no discursive space and perhaps little social need for other rights and/or other means of defining, deciding and enforcing disciplinary balances, and vice versa. Thus, insofar as, both before and after the promulgation of the Constitution, there was little in the way of other rights etc. to provide a counter to patriarchalism (for the persistence of conciliatory fora, for example, see Henderson, 1977, pp. 209 ff.), there was also little to stop patriarchalism from strongly reasserting itself at some future date. For a time it even seemed likely that ancient Chinese law would provide the model for Meiji jurists looking to the future (Chen, 1981).

As it happens an ancient but indigenous rather than Chinese concept, *jori*, did in fact provide the means whereby the traditional patriarchalism of the extended family or 'house' system maintained itself as the Meiji era progressed. *Jori* was extremely important during this period of rapid change because it referred to a source of law that could be invoked in the absence of positive or customary law. *Jori* is often translated as 'reason', but as Takayanagi (1976, pp. 175 ff.; see also, Noda, 1976, pp. 222–4) has convincingly argued it is perhaps better translated as 'common sense'. Its discursive effects may be best illustrated by quoting from a treatise by a very prominent and liberalistically inclined Meiji lawyer, which shows how patriarchalism maintained itself even within the very discourse of capitalist private property which otherwise might have been expected to have been its solvent:

> The issue of a law in 1872, which abolished the prohibition of sale of land and granted title deeds to landowners . . . and the establishment of joint-stock companies . . . mark[ed] the next step in the development

of the separate property of house members. The court of law began to recognise house members' separate property in title-deeds . . . and the like, which they held in their own names, and afterwards in other things also, when their separate titles could be proved.

In this manner individual property grew up within the house, that is to say, a house-member began to have his own property as an individual and not as a house-member. This change took place while the house-system was still in full vigour; and the consequence was that, the devolution of this new kind of property after the death of the owner resembled more the feudal escheat than succession. It did not descend to the children of the deceased, but ascended to the house-head.

(Hozumi, 1938, pp. 172–3)

Thus the presence of patriarchalist elements within legal discourse could prevent an owner, and one empowered as such by legislation issuing from the *tenno* himself, from deciding upon the dispositions to be made of his property after his death. However, it takes little imagination to appreciate that the effects of the same presence on the freedom available to the employees of such a property-owner were even more restrictive. Especially since in their regard, apart from an edict of 1872 establishing freedom of contract, neither positive nor customary law contained any other liberal ideas such as a right to freedom of association (Beer, 1984, pp. 46–53). Instead, Tokugawa prohibitions of peasant unions and collective bargaining were expressly continued (Marsland, 1989, pp. 29 ff.; Nakamura, 1962, p. 3.)

The Meiji Constitution of 1890 begins, 'The Empire of Japan shall be reigned over and governed by a line of Emperors unbroken for ages eternal.' The lawmaking power thus rather definitely rested in the hands of a *tenno*, whose prerogative, outside of the extensive areas entirely reserved to it (i.e. military, police, public welfare, constitutional revision and emergency powers), was constrained only by the need to request retroactive Diet approval for any uses of the lawmaking power that had not been so approved beforehand. Even the necessity of the Diet's approval of the budget represented little by way of a constraint on executive power, since the previous year's appropriation would stand again should the Diet not approve a new budget. The Diet itself consisted of two houses: an upper house of peers elected by and from the nobility and supplemented by imperial appointees and members of the *tenno's* family; and a lower house of representatives elected by the population at large according to a property-based franchise provided for in a separate piece of legislation, which had the effect of limiting the franchise to only a little over 1 per cent of the population.

Despite constitutional provision for an independent judiciary and guarantees of a long list of personal freedoms, the invented term *Staatrechts* (Statelaw) might be more descriptive of the legal realities in Japan prior to the defeat in the Pacific War than the term that, out of deference to the legal system's German inspiration, was actually used, namely *Rechtsstaat* (Law State). One reason why is suggested by the unintended humour present in the rather strained effort by Baron Ito, a member of the *genro* (council of elders) and chair of the constitutional drafting committee, to find a democratic significance in the use of the traditional phrase 'the great treasure' to describe the people. This culminates in the following quotation from a speech by an assistant chief of police on the occasion of a pardon: 'You must henceforth become the great treasure of the land, and must make ready to pay your taxes' (Ito, 1889, p. 35). More seriously, the legal primacy of the state's executive interest is apparent in such constitutional provisions as: the divinity of the sovereign; the uniquely extensive ordinance powers reserved to the *tenno* (Nakano, 1923, pp. 3, 6, 13, 18); and in the very restricted powers granted to the Diet. It is also apparent in: the limitations on the judiciary's powers in relation to the activities of the state; the absence of sanctions that the judiciary may exercise on its own behalf, such as the power to fine or jail for contempt (Haley, 1982a); and the qualified nature of most of the rights granted to the citizenry. The limitations on the judiciary's powers vis-à-vis the remainder of the state are clear from Article 61, which provides as follows:

> No suit at law, which relates to rights alleged to have been infringed by the illegal measures of the administrative authorities, and which shall come within the competency of the Court of Administrative Litigation specially established by law, shall be taken cognizance of by a Court of Law.

In his simultaneously published commentary Ito explained part of the somewhat cynical reasoning behind this limitation in the following terms: 'administrative expediency is just what judicial authorities are not ordinarily apt to be conversant with' (Ito, 1889, p. 110).

In what Beckmann (1957, p. 94) has aptly referred to as 'another repository of authoritarianism', the Constitution's 'bill of rights', only two of the rights are specified in an unqualified manner, that of freedom of abode and movement, and (presumably to satisfy the other parties to the 'unequal treaties') that of arrest and trial according to law. Each of the others, whether rights of privacy, property, religious belief, or speech and association (i.e. those most central to a democratic public sphere and the entrenchment of each other as well as of other citizenship rights) is qualified in their very promulgation by reference to the possibility of some limitations being imposed upon them by the passage of some later law. Again it is instructive to note the rationale given by Ito (1889, p. 55–6):

> as every one of these double-edged tools can easily be misused, it is necessary for the maintenance of public order, to punish by law and *prevent by police measures* delegated by law any disturbance . . . of the peace of the country.
>
> (emphasis added)

As a more liberal writer put it some twenty years later, 'There is nothing in the constitution to safeguard the rights and liberties of the people from the permanent executive officials' (Uyehara, 1910, p. 132).

In sum, Japan remained a 'theocratic-patriarchal' state (Hozumi, 1938, p. 86) even after the promulgation of the Constitution, and despite the plaudits proffered by the American Supreme Court Justice Oliver Wendell Holmes, and the British evolutionist sociologist Herbert Spencer. These plaudits are, of course, not surprising given that at the time there were also strict limits on the popular enjoyment of rights in Britain and the United States. Nor, unsurprisingly, need the accuracy of Uyehara's judgement be significantly challenged when one takes into account the various legal Codes that came into force in the following decade. This said, it might just have been otherwise in the area of private law, if the original, French-inspired Civil Code had come into force. The various books of this latter Code did in fact become law in the course of the year 1890, but a vigorous campaign was waged against it and, for rather different if equally mixed reasons, the accompanying Commercial Code. First, the Codes' dates of enforcement were postponed and then they were rewritten. The reasons for the campaign are made clear in the following paraphrase of an article by Hozumi Yatsuka (a very influential, contemporary conservative jurist):

> he vehemently took exception to the individualistic tone of the Civil Code . . . ; he emphasised the fact that the transplanting of the civil Code based on the principle of individualistic Christianity in this land founded on ancestor worship . . . not only ran counter to our time-honoured morals and manners, but also to the great principle of education and culture . . . revealed in the Imperial Rescript on Education.
>
> (Nakamura, 1962, p. 86, n. 15)

Here, the problem was, as Mukai and Toshitani (1967, p. 46) have put it, how to square the need for freedom in the relations between enterprises with the equally imperative need to respect the patriarchalist authority structure (i.e. the 'gentle ways and beautiful customs') within families and enterprises. On Nakamura's analysis (1962, pp. 90–2; see also Hozumi, 1938, pp. 173 ff.), such a campaign was unnecessary. The original Code gave ample support to the status aspects of patriarchalism, for example as they affected the honorific position of the head of the 'house'. The Civil Code was rewritten nevertheless and came into force in 1898. It strengthened patriarchal authority relative to the 'house'. In addition, although it reclassified leases as obligations rather than real rights and abolished certain customary, feudal rights in land (*usufruct*, use, domicile), it also allowed the validity of others such as *emphyteusis* (a grant of land for ever or a very long period upon condition that an annual rent was paid) – the latter for fifty years after the promulgation of the Code, regardless of whether or not the land was legally owned by another person (Ishii, 1968, pp. 577 ff.; Nakamura, 1962, pp. 98–100).

To most modern readers (Haley, 1982b, for example) the conservatism of the revised Code has been seen to lie in the limited nature of the restraints on capital that it contained, whereas from the present perspective it lay in the continued existence of any such restraints. Because of these restraints, although the Code contained a thoroughly modern definition of ownership (i.e. one that expressly protected the capitalist right to profit from the ownership of property), it cannot be said that the freedom of capital was the premise upon which the Code operated and therefore that it articulated a discourse different from and opposed to theocratic-patriarchalism. Read, as it had to be, in conjunction with the Constitution and, as it usually was, in the light of ultra-conservative commentaries on the latter such as Ito's (Pittau, 1967, p. 199), the Code did little to enhance capital's freedom:

> the right of property is under the powers of the state. It ought therefore to be subordinated to the latter.
>
> (Ito, 1889, p. 50)

> When it is necessitated by public benefit private individuals may be compelled *nolens volens* to part with their property.
>
> (ibid. p. 50)

It failed therefore to establish a substantial and individualistic discursive counterweight to patriarchalism or the *tenno*-state and not surprisingly, given that many capitalist Diet members, and not just farmers, were as vocal in their support for the postponement and rewriting of the Codes as the nobility.

All that said, the promulgation of the Constitution, the Codes and therefore the installation of the most basic machinery of liberal governance, nevertheless gave a measure of independence or, better, a method of gaining independence to the judiciary, even though the courts were understood to exercise juridical power only 'in the name of the emperor'. The judiciary quickly established a degree of independence in fact when, in 1891, it resisted government pressure for a more severe penalty than the law allowed in connection with an attempt on the life of the visiting Russian crown prince (Henderson, 1968b, pp. 424–6). Despite an understandable early pedagogical concern with exegetical discussions of the Codes (for the classic English language example, see De Becker's *Annotated Civil Code of Japan*, 1909), and despite a preference for very formalistic, 'black letter' techniques of interpretation, jurists and the judiciary gradually became more interpretatively active. They expanded and qualified the role anyway allowed them by the Constitution's continued, if more narrowly circumscribed, allowance of '*jori*' as a source of law (Henderson and Haley, 1978, p. 375). And they successfully claimed a place for their own precedents as a source of law (Itoh, 1970, pp. 779–85). This was sufficient to permit certain brave jurists to attempt to constrain the executive's power somewhat.

The most dramatic example of such an attempt was Tatsukichi Minobe's, for a time, widely accepted critique ('the organ theory') of the patriarchalist interpretation of the Constitution in the name of the rule of law (Miller, 1965). According to this critique, the office of *tenno* simply embodied the sovereign power of the state as a whole in its executive, legislative and judicial forms and hence was neither superior to its component institutions nor beyond their purview. On this basis Minobe argued that the tenno, even when exercising what might otherwise seem to be his reserved ordinance powers, not only could not impose his will on the other state institutions but also was himself subject to legislative and judicial constraint. However, as Banno (1987, pp. 9–10) has made clear, significantly, even Minobe had some difficulty reconciling his theory with the unambiguous nature of the tenno's position of military leadership. Nevertheless, this theory held sway amongst jurists until the 1930s. Then, like Minobe himself, it fell victim to the rising tide of militarism. As the amended Peace Preservation Law of 1941 stated, 'anyone who appears like they *might want* to change the absolutism of the emperor (was to be arrested)' (emphasis in the original, quoted in Beer, 1984, p. 66; see also Mitchell, 1976, pp. 201–5).

Thus the arrival of a *Rechtsstaat* ultimately failed to secure a more open public sphere let alone a freer private one. The public sphere remained too closed thanks to the limitations on the liberal-democratic freedoms, whilst the private sphere remained too open thanks to the aid given to the effectiveness of the state's surveillance and disciplinary powers by its continuing free access to the various registries (*koseki*) and their highly personal information which could be and was used to enrole heads of families in the disciplining of their kin (Henderson and Haley, 1978, p. 411). Both failures were accelerated by renewed state encouragement of conciliation (*chotei*) as an alternative to legal proceedings in the 1920s and 1930s (Haley, 1978, pp. 373–8). This began with the passage of the Land-Lease and House Lease Conciliation Law of 1922 and culminated with that of the Special Wartime Civil Affairs Law of 1942. This development continued and encouraged the restraints on capital in relation to the sale and use of land that the rewriting of the Constitution had achieved, adding to them substantial restrictions on the rights of creditors (Haley, 1982b, p. 138; Henderson, 1974, pp. 212–14), although presumably only in cases where the debtors were those, like farmers, of whom the state approved.

In sum, whether one prefers the term *Rechtsstaat* or *Staatrechts*, the *rechts* involved were clearly neither individualistic in any simple way, nor by the same token capable of offering much resistance to patriarchalism. Thus, insofar as the Constitution protected the freedom of the emperor-state to act as it pleased, and insofar as the new Codes repeated this protection, they perpetuated the presence of 'patriarchalism' within legal discourse. 'Skillfully interwoven' (Mukai and Toshitani, 1967, p. 46) though patriarchalism and capitalist right most definitely were in the two texts, this did not prevent the discourse they made possible from being unable to resist a resurgent patriarchalism in the 1930s.

CONCLUSION

To summarise the argument of Part I, when considered in the contexts of real rather than mythical nineteenth-century England and America as well as early twentieth-century Japan, the complex history of rights discourse as a potentially universal means of making capitalism even a stoically tolerable (in Moore's sense, see above p. 46) component of social life is not very encouraging let alone uplifting. In line with its paradoxical nature, rights discourse developed hand in hand, so to speak, with the machinery of power as part of what Foucault refers to as a 'complex strategical situation'. In eighteenth-century England rights at least protected the interests of nascent capitalists, if few others, but as part of a system of thought that we now call liberalism which grounded itself in fictitious understandings of the origins of human society – Locke's 'state of nature' – and English history – the mythic understandings of such texts and events as Magna Carta and the Glorious Revolution of 1688. In nineteenth and much of twentieth-century America, the federal Bill of Rights was inapplicable to state governments and courts, which was where citizens were most in need of it. Moreover, the more general discourse of liberty and rights placed the interests of full-grown capitalists at the centre of the legal cosmos on the grounds that it was thereby showing respect for the efforts of labour when it did not actually recognise any of labour's self-declared interests as in any sense rightful. And, finally, in Japan rights discourse, transmuted into the 'rule of law', enabled the Meiji state to regain its jurisdiction over foreigners in its own territory, but without granting any meaningful rights to its own people who therefore remained subjects rather than became citizens.

In sum and because of the social forces that produced it, the story of rights discourse up to the 1930s is a history of protection for the few and myths for the many. So why and how do we now, only some 75 years later, hold it in such high esteem? In keeping, once again, with the paradoxical character of rights discourse, the answers to these questions are perhaps unexpected and they begin where one would least expect them to – with establishment of the rule of (property) law. The Langdellians, the English textbook writers, and indeed the perhaps overly rationalistic continental European codifiers (Glenn, 2000, ch. 5) may all be criticised either for their mistaken conception of scientific method or for their less than rigorous application of it, depending upon one's own episte- mological position. However, equally, they all also demonstrated and enhanced the capacity of the law to make a difference in social life by their efforts on the one hand to define the leading concepts of legal discourse and on the other to specify the manner in which these concepts should be articulated with one another, or, in other words, by their efforts to create a new expert knowledge. Anticipations of the capacity of such expert knowledge to make a difference even under the unfavourable conditions obtaining in late nineteenth-century America and early twentieth-century Japan may be found both in Justice Holmes' famous dissents (Horwitz, 1992, ch. 4) and Minobe's 'Organ Theory' (see above, p. 72).

Horwitz oversimplified therefore when he argued in the first of his two already classic studies of the development of American law that the meaning of the transition from the earlier legal instrumentalism to the later 'legal formalism' was simply the completion of the law's problem-solving activities on behalf of property and the emergence of a consequent need to 'freeze' the legal advantages it had gained (Horwitz, 1977, ch. 8). In addition to any such freezing, the effect of the increasing formalisation of legal reason was, first, to provide judges and jurists more generally with a method for arriving at specifically legal solutions to the increasing number of new (that is, to them literally unprecedented) issues placed before them as a result of the ongoing processes of social change. And second, to make it at least possible that the law might yet be able to recognise the rights of the propertyless, the non-white and the female. Indeed the same points were made by Justice Holmes at the time:

> What has been said will explain the failure of all theories which consider the law only from its formal side, whether they attempt to deduce the corpus from a priori postulates, or fall into the humbler error of supposing the science of the law to reside in the *elegantia juris*, or logical cohesion of part with part. The truth is, that the law is always approaching, and never reaching, consistency. It is forever adopting new principles from life at one end, and it always retains old ones from history at the other, which have not yet been absorbed or sloughed off. It will become entirely consistent only when it ceases to grow.
>
> (quoted in Gilmore, 1977, p. 53)

I would add, however, that it was nevertheless ultimately the recognition by the other branches of government of the law's entitlement to use its expert knowledge in the pursuit of consistency that eventually enabled judges to act on new principles and even some old ones in the case of the Bill of Rights. This, at least, will be the argument of the following chapter.

II

RIGHTING THE WORLD?

7

THE UNITED STATES AND THE INVENTION OF HUMAN RIGHTS

This part will be concerned with what Kirsten Sellars (2002) has termed, somewhat ironically, the 'rise and rise' of human rights in the post-1945 period. Chapters 7, 8 and 9 will focus on how rights re-emerged from the shadow of Dicey's version of the rule of law in western Europe and, especially, the United States to become central to the formation of the UN. Chapter 10 will describe post-1946 developments in Japan, which are widely regarded as demonstrating both the possibility, and the beneficial effects, of introducing rights discourse into non-western societies. And finally, Chapter 11 will begin by outlining the philosophical resistance to any reformulation of human rights discourse before describing the major challenges that it faces today. The chapter ends by showing how these challenges have transformed the sociological approach to human rights.

In western Europe and Britain's settler colonies, the revival of rights was very much a political story but one with two discordant but nevertheless complementary aspects. The first aspect concerned the rise of what Marshall termed social rights as either social-democratic parties took power or liberal and conservative parties tried to outbid them in pursuit of working-class votes. Few other Europeans in the late 1940s used Marshall's terminology, largely because of the mutual antipathy between the supporters of rights discourse and the labour movement. The property-centredness of the first group's position meant that, following Dicey, it considered such ideas as labour or welfare rights to be self-contradictory (Hayek, 1944), whilst the state-centredness of the second group's programme led to them preferring the term welfare state to describe what they had either achieved or desired. The second aspect concerned the rise of fascism and the belated horror at its appalling crimes against humanity. These events galvanised, first, western public opinion, causing H.G. Wells, for example, to write a new version of Paine's *The Rights of Man*, and latterly the United States government to lead the effort both to construct the United Nations and to develop the more socially and politically inclusive conception of rights which it labelled 'human rights'. In this context, then, Marshall's famous essay of 1949 may be seen with hindsight as an effort to reconnect socialist or welfarist discourse with a resurgent rights tradition emanating from the United States.

The Western-European aspect of the story of the revival of rights discourse has been told sociologically and very well many times already, notably in the texts mentioned earlier by Marshall, Stephens, Esping-Anderson and Mann, plus the many studies of the growth of citizenship rights and the welfare state. Again, rather than repeat what I am assuming is a very familiar story, I will focus on the revival of rights discourse in my two outlier states, the United States and Japan. This is both because these parts of the story are far less widely known, and because of their importance to the main story – the United States was the driving force behind the global revival of rights discourse and Japan represents the principal test case with respect to the discourse's effectiveness in non-western societies. The question that will guide my account of American developments is: 'How was it possible for the United States to become and, until recently, remain the driving force behind the human rights project, given its defining nineteenth-century commitment to a rather narrow, property-centred conception of liberty?' The question that will guide my account of Japanese developments will be: 'How was it possible that Japan became and has remained committed to human rights, despite the continuing power of patriarchalist or, nowadays, familialist discourse within that society?'

THE REVIVAL OF RIGHTS DISCOURSE IN THE UNITED STATES

It was the dramatic realignment of political forces represented by the switch of the Northern labour vote from the Republicans to Roosevelt's Democrats following the 1929 Wall Street Crash that ushered in the New Deal and made the revival of rights discourse in the United States a reality.

However, the story of the revival begins some years earlier in the law schools: that is, in the space for the generation of expertise and power created by the formalists. The scholars who took advantage of this space to criticise their formalist benefactors and so create the legal conditions within which a broadening of the constituency of rights bearers could occur latterly became known as the Legal Realists. This very loosely structured school of thought had its roots in antebellum juridical instrumentalism – a movement which Langdellianism had erased from juristic memory in all but a few cases, amongst them Justice Holmes' (White, 1976, ch. 8). Because of this erasure, Realism is usually described as a new and very twentieth-century phenomenon within which Roscoe Pound's sociology was blended with such ingredients as: Justice Holmes' dissents (Hunt, 1978); Louis Brandeis' briefs (White, 1976, ch. 8); Arthur Corbin's *Contracts* (1950); Justice Cardozo's judgments (White, 1976, ch. 12); and Karl Llewellyn's treatises (Twining, 1973). Despite their numerous disagreements, these jurists were united in their belief that the law at the time decided questions in the way described by Holmes in the notorious 'due process' case of *Lochner* v. *New York* (1905), in which a state law limiting the hours of bakery workers to 60 hours per week was declared unconstitutional; that is, 'upon an economic theory [laissez-faire liberalism], which a large part of the country does not entertain'. More positively, they also agreed with Holmes' assertion, in his famous text, *The Common Law*, that: 'The life of the law has not been logic: it has been experience . . . the law finds its philosophy [in] the nature of human needs'.

The difference between Holmes and the more self-conscious Realists was that for the most part the latter were much more enthusiastic about state-sponsored attempts to acknowledge the rightfulness of a wider variety of such needs. Where Holmes tolerated such attempts, the Realists welcomed and encouraged them; and where Holmes thought that the legislature had to have constitutional priority over the judiciary, the Realists thought that the legislature *should have* such priority. Both wings of the movement recognised, however, the need for some reorganisation of the relationships between the separate institutions of the state. Ostensibly, the Realists claimed that it mattered little that the legislative floodgates they thereby opened spelt the end of juridical consistency. One of their number, Jerome Frank (1930), even argued that to insist that the law should be consistent and rational in the face of many different and divergent human needs was childish in the Freudian sense that it betrayed a need for a father figure inappropriate in an 'adult jurist'.

However, despite their rejection of the idea that what gave law whatever consistency it possessed was the fact that it was based on logical deduction from inductively produced principles, the Realists nevertheless believed that it should be possible to predict the outcomes of particular cases. The bases for such predictions could not be the black letters of the law alone, but had, realistically, to include knowledge of the motives, interests and social positions of those who write and interpret the black letters. The suggestion that the law as a sphere of activity could be social-scientifically predictable but in itself unprincipled was, not surprisingly, neither particularly popular outside the universities, nor for long unchallenged within them (Purcell, 1973, ch. 9). Realism was castigated as a 'Jurisprudence of Despair' (Mecham, 1936), and its disruptive discursive consequences were strongly countered by the commencement of the neo-formalist but relatively modest efforts at codification represented by the 'Restatement' project that commenced in the 1920s (Gilmore, 1977, pp. 72–4; Schwartz, 1974, p. 210). Nevertheless, Realism contributed greatly to the reordering of legal discourse that occurred during the New Deal (1932–9). Not only, then, did Realism undermine the pretensions of Langdellianism and enhance thereby the claims of the legislature relative to the judiciary, but it also documented the changes that were occurring within key concepts – the changes that explain why the reordering that occurred during the New Deal was accurately described in a title of a book by Edward Corwin (1941): *Constitutional Revolution Ltd*.

As was shown in the previous chapter, 'property' became the generative concept in Formalist legal discourse, and it is therefore fitting that this outline of the Formalists' decline should start by discussing the possibilities opened up by the continuing developments within and around the concept of property. The developments of interest here are, ironically, those that in the previous chapter were represented as the apogee of property's dominance. As the social and political context changed, these developments took on a different significance that drew attention to their obverse side. Although the fact that property came to signify intangible as well as corporeal relations undoubtedly enhanced the substantive power of property owners in a direct fashion, especially vis-à-vis labour, indirectly and discursively it created the possibility of property's constraint and labour's belated assertion of its First Amendment rights. That is, once property came to be seen as a bundle of distinguishable rights (see above, p. 57) rather than an organic unity, it became possible to think about qualifying some of these rights while arguably not destroying private property as such. According to Wesley Hohfeld's (1919) study of the pertinent case law, no rights, including property right, rested on a simple liberty but in fact typically comprised a bundle of variously established: 'liberties' to perform certain actions; 'claims' or expectations vis-à-vis specified others; 'powers' that allow legal subjects to assume certain specified roles and change certain social relations; and 'immunities' against prosecution and/or civil suit when pursuing ends that are otherwise defined as illegal. The critical and reformist thought made possible by Hohfeld's work gained particular, and eventually legislative, force where the property owner was a corporation, and where it was possible to argue that there was a 'public interest' in such action.

In a similar manner, changes in the law of contract gradually undermined the inviolability of freedom of contract. Corbin had long contended privately that no coherent contractual doctrine had ever been actually enforced by American courts and that the existence of such a doctrine was a figment of the Langdellian imagination. However, it was not until he began teaching and writing to this effect in the early twentieth century that doctrinal notice was taken of this fact (Gilmore, 1974, ch. 3). Corbin demonstrated that the 'operative facts' were at least as important as legal doctrine in determining the outcome of a case. His study of Cardozo's judgments in New York, for example, showed how a concern to achieve justice could mean that such facts resulted in significant changes of doctrine. Corbin's view of the judicial process was confirmed by Cardozo (1920) himself and had results that were, in a sense, eventually written into law, since Corbin was also one of the principle authors of the partial antidote to his own Realism, namely *The Restatement of Contracts* (1932). Gilmore has described the ultimate consequences of the decline of contract as an 'explosion of liability' on the grounds of negligence:

> Speaking descriptively, we might say that what is happening is that 'contract' is being reabsorbed into the mainstream of 'tort'. Until the general theory of contract was hurriedly run up late in the nineteenth century, tort had always been our residual category of civil liability. As the contract rules dissolve, it is becoming so again. It should be pointed out that the theory of tort into which contract is being reabsorbed is itself a much more expansive theory of liability than was the theory of tort from which contract was artificially separated a hundred years ago.
>
> (Gilmore, 1974, p. 87)

The change that Gilmore (1974, pp. 60 ff.) emphasises was that represented by Section 90 of *The Restatement of Contracts*, which contains the idea of 'promissory estoppel', and which allows a court, where it considers such action would benefit a weaker party, to equate reliance on an offer of work, for example, with a monetary deposit. Promissory estoppel, then, allows a court to enforce contractual liability where there would otherwise be no such liability. The general discursive significance of such changes was not simply that contract began to dissolve back into torts and its general but ever more complexly elaborated principles of negligence and 'duty of care', but also that the possession and protection of rights depended no more on the possession of a 'proper' contract than it did on the possession of corporeal property. In this way, it became possible to think that, like property right, freedom of contract need not pre-empt all labour or citizenship rights, since rights need not originate in either property or contract but might either be found by the courts in other areas of the law or even be created by the state. This again was a thought that gained force, and eventually legislative force, as the labour contractor ceased to be an individual and became a corporation and, again, as it became clear that there was a 'public interest' in legislation that granted rights to those possessing neither property nor explicit contractual entitlements.

What rounded off the Realists'contribution to the revival of rights discourse, and therefore allowed the separate but interactive effects of the changes to property and contract to come to fruition, was the Realists' simultaneous support for the enhanced 'police power' of the state. This enhancement was the product of a separate set of developments from that already discussed which gradually allowed 'the public interest' to gain legal force and so create what Arthur Miller has called 'the positive state' (1968, pp. 76 ff.; see also Hurst, 1977, ch.2). The comparatively very belated activation of the 'police power', then, was what gradually enabled legislative force to be given to three doctrinally created possibilities: first, the possibility that property rights were qualifiable in ways that were not necessarily in violation of due process (*vide*, the Sherman Act of 1890 which outlawed monopolistic practices on the part of corporations); second, the possibility that freedom of contract need not pre-empt all labour rights (*vide*, the several turn-of-the-century state laws restricting hours of work and conditions of employment for women and children); and third, the possibility that tortious liability did not have to depend on proof of fault (*vide* the various early twentieth-century state workmen's compensation acts). Moreover, in sum and as a consequence of its use in the Social Security Act Cases (1937), the emergence of the police power was what all but destroyed the system so beloved by the Langdellian formalists.

As Miller (1968, p. 84) has put it, the rise of the 'positive state' was the development that changed the Constitution from one of 'limitations to one of powers' and so made possible the arrival of America's minimalist welfare state – pensions, unemployment benefits, income support for the disabled, the very old and the children of one-parent families, but no general right to health care or income support – in that the Supreme Court used the concept of the 'police power' to reject claims that the Social Security Act (1935) the established these programmes was unconstitutional. The significance of these rejections has been well put by Bernard Schwartz (1974, p. 165):

> The significance of the Social Security Act Cases, however, extends far beyond the statute at issue. The opinions delivered furnished the doctrinal basis for the developing state. That state was characterized above all by the geometric growth of government largess. 'Government is a gigantic siphon. It draws in revenue and power, and pours forth wealth: money, benefits, services, contracts, franchises, and licenses' (Reich, 1974, p. 733). The field of benefactions came to occupy an increasingly large proportion of the efforts of government. The political order itself was compendiously called the welfare state. The key instrument of the welfare state is the fisc, its motive force the power of the purse. The 1937 decisions construed that power most broadly. If Congress chooses to tax and spend to operate schemes of old age benefits and unemployment insurance, that is a matter within its discretion. 'For the past six years the nation unhappily, has been placed in a position to learn at first hand the nature and extent of the problem of unemployment, and to appreciate its profound influence upon the public welfare' (*Carmichael* v. *Southern Coal Co.*, 1937, p. 515).

As a result of the Social Security Act Cases, it became possible to make use of a further form of state power, namely that of the purse, for whatever social purpose the legislature might decide on. The only restriction on this power specified in the Constitution is that it should be exercised 'to . . . provide for the common Defence and general Welfare'. The net effect of the Social Security Act Cases, then, was to allow the legislature to determine whether a given exercise of the power of the purse would promote the general welfare: 'The line must still be drawn between one welfare and another, between particular and general . . . There is a middle ground or certainly a penumbra in which discretion is at large. That discretion, however, is not confided to the courts. The discretion belongs to Congress' (*Helvering* v. *Davis*, 1937, pp. 640–1). The arrival of a set of rights for labour was a much more complicated matter that I have described in detail elsewhere (Woodiwiss, 1990b) but they too were confirmed in 1937 when the Wagner Act of 1935 was accepted by the Supreme Court as a constitutional expansion of the First Amendment right to freedom of association.

This completes my outline of the rather particular legal changes and institutional reorderings that, in the course of the 1930s, allowed the displacement of property and the judiciary by a revival of a broader rights discourse and the legislature at the centre of American law. The result was the democratisation of the rule of law so that it ceased to be a guarantor of the privileging of private property and instead became simply a shorthand way of saying that 'those who exercise power over others must have legal authority for their action' (Ewing and Gearty, 2000, p. 12). The ending of the war against fascism saw the United States take the lead in an attempt to embed the recently invented idea of human rights within the new system of global security that it sought to establish and which ultimately became known as the United Nations. Thus the wider significance of the story that has just been outlined is that the very form, and much of the content, of the purportedly universal moral and political discourse what we now call human rights originated in the rather unusual set of local, American developments allowed or made necessary by a very particular set of social and political circumstances.

THE INVENTION OF HUMAN RIGHTS

International human rights law is a subdivision of international law which makes, or should make, it a deeply suspect enterprise in that international law has long been characterised by the pre-emption of the possibility of a global consensus by the prior formation of a western one. Thus, although in theory the most venerable source of international law is 'international custom' or the ways in which states customarily relate to one another (see the discussion of cosmopolitanism above, p. 12), in practice the states concerned have been limited to western or western-like states. Thus, in the nineteenth century, the 'unequal treaties' between various western and non-colonised Asian states (see above, p. 62) were justified by reference to the 'law of nations' which prohibited any interference with trade and communication between nations (Seizelet, 1992, p. 61). Indeed many western nations considered themselves to have been rather generous in drawing up such treaties since they harboured serious doubts about whether or not non-western nations were covered by international law because of their non-Christian character. Moreover, the issue was only 'settled' in 1874, when the Paris Institute of International Law decided that non-western nations could claim legal equality with their western equivalents under international law provided they conformed to what the West defined as the 'universal principles of civilisation' – hence the necessity of the Meiji Constitution and Codes in Japan (ibid., p. 63) if the 'unequal treaties' were to be renegotiated.

Unsurprisingly in view of this background, but also largely unacknowledged because of ignorance of it, the same pre-emption of a global consensus by a western one occurred with respect to human rights law. In her recent and stimulatingly iconoclastic book, Kirsten Sellars (2002) correctly takes to task all those who regard the idea of human rights as an ancient one rooted in many highly diverse cultures. However, she herself locates the idea's source in the European Enlightenment which spawned the eighteenth-century bills of rights; that is, in what Kant termed republicanism rather than in the *ius cosmopoliticum* (see above, p. 13). Thus she misses the significance of the shift, following apparently already established Latin American usage (Glendon, 2003), from talking of either 'natural rights' or the 'rights of man' to 'human rights' that occurred in President Roosevelt's 'Four Freedoms' speech of 6 January 1941. This significance was that the shift involved not just a verbal change but a change of reference too. Thus, whilst freedoms one and two – those of expression and religion – as well as the more obviously patriotic sections of the speech, clearly referred to the major tradition and what Hohfeld referred to as liberties or immunities, freedoms three and four – from want and fear – equally clearly referred through the principle of reciprocity to the minor tradition, to the idea of a global 'community of the land . . . a community of reciprocal action', and to what Hohfeld referred to as powers and claims rather than liberties.

That said, this ambiguity is much clearer in the 'Four Freedoms' speech than in the later and already cold war-affected UDHR. The speech ended as follows:

In the future days which we seek to make secure, we look forward to a world founded upon four essential human freedoms.

The first is freedom of speech and expression – everywhere in the world.

The second is freedom of every person to worship God in his own way – everywhere in the world.

The third is freedom from want, which, translated into world terms, means economic understandings which will secure to every nation a healthy peacetime life for its inhabitants – everywhere in the world.

The fourth is freedom from fear, which, translated into world terms, means a world-wide reduction of armaments to such a point and in such a thorough fashion that no nation will be in a position to commit an act of physical aggression against any neighbor – anywhere in the wold.

That is no vision of a distant millennium. It is a definite basis for a kind of world attainable in our own time and generation. That kind of world is the very antithesis of the so-called 'new order' of tyranny which the dictators seek to create with the crash of a bomb.

To that new order we oppose the greater conception – the moral order. A good society is able to face schemes of world domination and foreign revolutions alike without fear.

Since the beginning of our American history we have been engaged in change, in a perpetual, peaceful revolution, a revolution which goes on steadily, quietly, adjusting itself to changing conditions without the concentration camp or the quicklime in the ditch. The world order which we seek is the cooperation of free countries, working together in a friendly, civilized society.

This nation has placed its destiny in the hands, heads and hearts of its millions of free men and women, and its faith in freedom under the guidance of God. Freedom means the supremacy of *human rights* everywhere.

(emphasis added)

What makes the fact that human rights discourse combines references to both the major and minor rights traditions critical is that it explains why the very idea of human rights remains both globally supported and contested. This is because, at the deepest discursive level, there is uncertainty about what the world would have to look like for even the aspirations represented by the present array of human rights to be realisable. Thus, as will become clear below, the history of human rights discourse in the UN is a history of a battle between a later and increasingly parochial, autonomy-centred, American reading of the discourse's possibilities whose authors have more and more stridently insisted on its universalism, and a literally cosmopolitan series of readings emanating from the remainder of the globe and stressing variants of the reciprocity principle, which have been systematically marginalised as cultural relativisms.

The founding text of the UN was its Charter which, despite the desires of some of its initial signatories, says very little about human rights except that they are important, to be promoted by the UN's Economic and Social Council (ECOSOC), and advanced by international co-operation.[1] In 1946, ECOSOC established a Commission on Human Rights, most of whose members were diplomats, which was charged with drawing up the UDHR. As Johannes Morsink (1999) has shown in considerable detail, the referential ambiguity of the discourse continued to mark the elaboration of the four freedoms that became the UDHR. However, the differences between capitalism and communism rather obviously came to overshadow and for a long time obscure the differences between the republican and cosmopolitan visions.

Thus there is little mention in the UDHR of the 'economic understandings which will secure to every nation a healthy peacetime life for its inhabitants – everywhere in the world'. Moreover, of the 24 specific human rights listed (Articles, 3–26), 18 may be defined as civil and political (see Articles 3–16 and 18–21), six of which concern rights in relation to legal authorities, whilst the remaining six may be defined as economic and social rights that are both inspired by the principle of reciprocity and compatible with private property ownership. More concretely, these rights projected a very western image of what Roosevelt had termed the 'good society' as one in which: private property is sacrosanct (Article 17); the rule of law securely established; the polity liberal-democratic; and a broad array of social services, voluntary associations, and legal statuses were already in existence – specifically, social security in all its forms (health, housing, unemployment and old-age insurance, income support and special protection for mothers and children), education, labour administration, trade unions and employment contracts.

Unsurprisingly, the Soviet Union and four of its allies, plus South Africa and Saudi Arabia, abstained when the Universal Declaration was put to the vote in the General Assembly. They did so because, given the ethical principles to which they were committed, as well as the ethical blind spots that are stressed in today's histories, they felt that it laid too much stress on the civil and political or, in Kantian terms, the republican side. For this reason, reflecting this division and their diplomatic backgrounds, the members of the Human Rights Commission, who included representatives of the abstaining states, took up a position best summarised as 'see no evil, hear only a little about any evil, and definitely do not speak of any evil.' That is, between 1946 and 1967 and because it disingenuously claimed to have no such power, the sole body then charged with the task of interrogating states concerning their human rights records, refused to investigate any complaints, agreed only to receive very general descriptions of alleged violations for research purposes, and instead concerned itself with preparing legislation in the form of the later Covenants. Thus the Human Rights Commission spent the six years from 1946 to 1954 working on what became the two principal Human Rights treaties (that is, for signatories, the two principal, positive sources of international law in the human rights area): the International Covenant on Civil and Political Rights (ICCPR) and the International Covenant on Economic, Social and Cultural Rights (ICESCR).

CONCLUSION

This chapter has outlined the re-emergence of rights discourse from the shadow created by late nineteenth-century understandings of the nature of the rule of law, according to which all other rights were subordinated to those of property unless they could be articulated in contractual terms. Thus, for example in Britain and the United States, the freedoms of speech and association were limited by the fact that, although in the absence of contrary positive legislation one could argue for, and organise in pursuit of, almost any cause, the outcome could not be, for example, any qualification of property right.

In western Europe, the challenging of this hierarchisation of rights was a turbulent, sometimes horrendously violent and always highly political process centred on the rise of nationalist and socialist ideologies and movements. In very different ways and on the basis of very different conceptions of social belonging, both of these movements rejected the individualistic assumptions upon which this hierarchisation rested. And they did so in the name of community, in the name, therefore, of some variant of the principle of reciprocity. In the extreme forms of these rejections exemplified by Communism and Fascism rights became practically meaningless since, whilst they continued to exist on paper, they could always be trumped by the interests of the state speaking in the name of the community. However, in the less extreme forms exemplified by Social and Christian Democracy, the principal of reciprocity found expression in a broadening of rights discourse that allowed the qualification of property rights in the names of need, reciprocity and the welfare state (Mauss, 1924; Titmuss, 1959, 1987).

In the United States, the challenge to the hierarchisation of rights represented by the late nineteenth-century conception of the rule of law developed more slowly, less violently and on the basis of as much legal as political input. Thus Realist jurists were able to take advantage of the intellectual autonomy established by the Formalists who had produced the property-centred conception of the rule of law in order to challenge the same conception. That is, modes of reasoning that had been initially developed to create the property-centred system were turned against the same system and used to create space within it for rights inspired by the principle of reciprocity. This reversal changed the significance of the law as a mode of governance insofar as some of the Realist jurists were judges themselves or at least influential on them, and with the result that some space for such rights was created within legal discourse itself. Latterly, the same reversal also provided techniques and strategies for use by Roosevelt's

New Deal Administrations as they legislated to fill the space created by the jurists with further very mildly chthonically-inspired rights. Reflecting the different social-structural and therefore political context as compared to the western European context, as well indeed as the greater role of legal reason in the process of constructing them, these new rights were both narrower in range than in western Europe and specified in such a way – that is, with the stress firmly on self-reliance rather than reciprocity – as to be far less of a challenge to the ideological and legal primacy of property (Woodiwiss, 1993, ch. 1). Nevertheless, when Roosevelt gave his 'Four Freedoms' speech of 1941, in which the term 'human rights' first appeared, the chthonic elements in his rights talk had a domestic referent even if their international referent soon proved illusory, at least as far as what we now call the global South was concerned.

In sum, despite significant differences in the breadth and terms of their rights discourses, but thanks to their shared revulsion at the appalling crimes of the Nazis, western European countries and the United States had developed similar conceptions of rights as being largely related to issues of personal freedom to do certain things and freedom from certain problems (Berlin, 1969). Thus it was relatively easy for them to agree on both the necessity and content of the UDHR. It was similarly easy for the already independent southern countries involved in the drafting and discussion of the UDHR to agree, since at that time their rights discourses were mainly derived directly from western Europe or, the case of the Philippines, the United States and did not yet bear any marks of their own more chthonic indigenous cultures. Much of the rest of the chthonically-inclined world was excluded from the preparation of the UDHR because it was colonised, which left only a few socialist and Islamic states, plus China, to put the case for reciprocity. This they did, but as Morsink shows but does not stress, they were *only* successful to the extent that their suggestions overlapped with western rights discourse, hence the abstention of several of these states from the vote in the General Assembly. In other words, like much of the rest of international law, the founding text of international human rights law represents yet another instance of the pre-emption of the possibility of a global consensus by a western one; and like rights discourse generally, the UDHR replicates the discourse's paradoxical character in that it too has turned out to offer protection only on the basis of the acceptance of inequality, this time on a global scale.

8

THE WARREN COURT
Setting the international human rights agenda

In order that the profundity of the American influence on the development of human rights in the UN should be understood, I will now return to the story of rights in the United States before continuing the UN story. Because of the ongoing consequences of the American social-structural particularities outlined above (see p. 51) and therefore the continuing absence of a social-democratic party capable of forming a government, the New Deal represented the high water mark for the revival of reciprocity in the form of social rights in the United States, save for the neap tide briefly represented by the 'War on Poverty' in the 1960s.

Between 1949 and 1960 the country was governed by a Republican Party that only grudgingly accepted the legitimacy of the New Deal's minimalist social rights, largely on the basis of electoral calculations, and was certainly not prepared to sponsor any extension or enhancement of them. Thus it fell to the Supreme Court to respond to any demands and campaigns for the extension or enhancement of rights (Epps, 1998). The Warren Court, as the Supreme Court came to be known between the 1950s and 1970s after its chief Justice, Earl Warren, is famous for its pro-rights stance. Indeed the United States owes the major part of its international reputation as a champion of rights discourse to the decisions of the Warren Court, especially as they related to the civil rights of African-Americans. Certainly the Warren Court was more solicitous of the rights of non-property owners than any of its predecessors had been or successors would be. However, its record is not unmixed, even with regard to civil rights. The general direction of the Warren Court's 'activism' was towards a more inclusive and expanded conception of individual liberty that continued the attenuated variant of reciprocity which I have elsewhere (Woodiwiss, 1993) termed Social Modernism. According to Social Modernism, individuals were expected to be self-reliant, could seek the help of 'responsible unions', but could expect state help only where their problems were not of their own making but the results of either certain physical/social disabilities (blindness, fatherlessness and old age) or, eventually, discrimination, provided that they remained loyal to the state. What I will call the Court's 'managerialism' constrained the same expanded liberty, especially where the Court considered the nation's security to be at stake. In a striking anticipation of today's illiberal climate, liberty was compromised disturbingly easily by being made conditional upon demonstrable loyalty. Hence the decision of the National Association for the Advancement of Colored People (NAACP) to give up the pursuit of economic and social rights on the grounds that they were widely regarded as Soviet-inspired (Anderson, 2003).

Schwartz (1974, p. 237) has argued that:

> there were three principal developments in the Warren Court regarding the protection of personal rights: (1) acceptance of the preferred position theory; (2) extension of the trend towards holding Bill of Rights guarantees binding on the states; and (3) broadening of the substantive content of the rights themselves.

Although it will be emphasised against such as Schwartz that the Warren Court was equally instrumental in constraining individual liberties rights and so was concerned to elaborate a rather specific conception of them, his classification of the pertinent enabling developments in public law will nevertheless serve to order the present discussion. 'Preferred position' theory was first stated by Justice Stone in 1938 and it argued that if the 'judicial activism' instanced by the infamous decision in *Lochner* v. *New York* (see above, p. 81) should ever be revived, the 'preferred' occasions would be those where the weight of the Constitution was thought to be necessary for the protection of personal rights. Under Chief Justice Warren this is precisely what was thought to be the case (for a contrary view see, Berger, 1977).

Amongst the Bill of Rights guarantees that were, extraordinarily belatedly, made binding on the states by the Warren Court were those relating to defendants in criminal cases, which protected them from double jeopardy and self-incrimination, as well as assured them a speedy jury trial and access to the possibility of bail. The culmination of this development was the promulgation of what became known as the 'Miranda Rules', according to which the admissibility of a confession was made dependent upon the police being able to demonstrate that they had warned the defendant that she or he had both the right to remain silent and to have a lawyer present (Bickel, 1970). The other federal level rights extended by the Warren Court to citizens vis-à-vis the states were those relating to freedom of the press, freedom to criticise public figures and freedom of association. The Court's actions in relation to freedom of expression will be discussed below, since its judgments were particularly ambiguous in their significance.

The substantiveness of the rights just discussed was also broadened by a number of decisions, *Brown* v. *Board of Education* (1954), *Baker* v. *Carr* (1962) and *Griffin* v. *Illinois* (1956), which sought to ensure equality of condition with respect to the enjoyment of constitutional liberties to African-American people, citizens living in urban areas and defendants in criminal trials respectively. The first decision initiated the process of racial desegregation, the second the reapportionment of congressional seats between the states so as to assure fair representation, and the third the introduction of a Public Defender system that ensured that all defendants had access to counsel.

In private law, the Court's 'activism' with respect to improving the substantiveness of individual rights was much slower to develop and only really became explicit in the late 1960s and early 1970s. Even so, during the 1950s and 1960s, the process of inserting 'public interest' considerations into the private law that had begun before the New Deal continued to develop. Thus the Court moved towards: with regard to contract, restricting freedom of contract in order to protect what were deemed to be weaker parties; in the area of tort, the socialisation of compensation for injuries; and finally, with regard to property owners and corporations, some qualification of their prerogatives by insisting that they give some consideration to the rights of individuals (Schwartz, 1974, chs 7, 9).

It is not, of course, surprising that the Court's 'activism' should have been so muted in the area of private law. In spite of the fact that this is the area in which the Court has most autonomy, it remained on this, as on the racial desegregation issue, particularly sensitive to the rights of property owners and the jurisdictions of other state agencies. There are two particularly noteworthy instances of this sensitivity, one relating to contract law and the other relating to labour law. The Court acquiesced to the decline of actual 'contracts' in inter-business relationships, which, where they remained, tended to contain arbitration clauses that precluded the taking of disputes to court. Thus, the main part of the court system's involvement with contract law became the enforcement of hire-purchase obligations etc., so that 'civil courts . . . (came to serve) as expensive adjuncts of . . . local finance companies' (Schwartz, 1974, pp. 279 ff). Labour law was, by contrast, the one area which provided an exception to the Court's general 'restraint' with respect to the improvement of the substantiveness of individual rights in the domain of private law. According to Martin Shapiro (1964, p. 75), fully one tenth of the Court's decisions in the years 1958–63 related to labour law cases. Through these decisions the Court acted to reduce the autonomy and constrain the collectivism of unions to an extent that provides a striking contrast to its indulgent treatment of corporations (Woodiwiss, 1990b, ch. 8).

For all that the actions of the Supreme Court just mentioned had as their explicit rationale the bolstering of individual liberty, they also had an implicit effect which was arguably of at least equal long term significance. The nature of this effect has been very well described by Alexander Bickel (1970, p. 104):

> In the Warren era . . . a tendency was noticeable to circumscribe and displace private ordering, to legalise society, to rationalise it in the sense in which the great industrial consolidators spoke of rationalising the economy, to impose order on norms, values and institutions. There was evidence . . . of an imperfectly bridled managerial drive.

One would be hard put to provide a better description of the managerialist nature of the Court's conception of private rights. The clearest demonstration of the Court's ambiguity towards freedom of expression – *the* core right in current American human rights discourse – and, therefore, of the effect of the Court's managerial effort arises from a consideration of its now long-forgotten but still influential decisions concerning the civil rights of members and alleged members or supporters of the Communist Party.

THE 'COMMUNIST PARTY CASES'

These cases fall into three groups. The Communist Party cases proper arose as a result of appeals against convictions that had been obtained under the Smith Act (1940) and the McCarran Act (1950). The Smith Act made it an offence to advocate in speech or writing 'the overthrowing or destroying (of) any government in the United States by force or violence', or to 'organise any society, group or assembly' dedicated to this end. Closely related to this first group of cases was a second group in which the Supreme Court had to decide whether or not the defence involved in the first Smith Act case had been in contempt of court during the trial, and more generally whether or not lawyers who refused to swear loyalty oaths could be prevented from practising. Finally, there was a group of cases in which the Court reviewed Congress' investigatory powers as represented by such as Senator Eugene McCarthy's House Un-American Activities Committee (HUAC).

Perhaps the clearest statement of the managerialist approach to freedom of expression that the Court developed in the first set of cases occurred in Justice Frankfurter's separate but concurring opinion in *Dennis et al.* (1951), where he stated that:

> Freedom of expression is the wellspring of our civilisation – the civilisation we seek to maintain and further by recognising the right of Congress to put some limitation on expression. Such are the paradoxes of life.

The containing purpose behind such statements was recognised in Justice Black's dissent where he argued that since the petitioners had done nothing more than 'agreed to assemble and talk and to publish certain ideas at a later date', the decision amounted to 'prior censorship of speech and press, which I believe the First Amendment forbids', (ibid., p. 40). In addition, he pointed out that the majority had actually 'jettisoned' the doctrine of 'clear and present danger', on which they claimed to base their decision, since they had stretched and relativised it out of all recognition by their interpretation of the phrase 'as speedily as possible' and their references to the world situation. Justice Douglas, the other dissenter, repeated Justice Black's arguments but added a prescient gloss of his own, which must have sounded, and indeed was, very sophisticated in the early 1960s:

> Full and free discussion keeps a society from becoming stagnant and unprepared for the stresses and strains that work to tear all civilisations apart . . . In days of trouble and confusion when bread lines were long, when the unemployed walked the streets, when people were starving, the advocates of a short cut by revolution might have had a chance to gain adherents. But today there are no such conditions. The country is not in despair; the people know Soviet Communism; the doctrine of

Soviet Revolution is exposed in all its ugliness and the American people want none of it.

The general consequences of this line of decisions was best summarised in Justice Douglas' dissent to the *Scales* decision (1961), when he said:

[it makes] serious Mark Twain's light-hearted comment that 'it is by the goodness of God that in our country we have those three unspeakably precious things:freedom of speech, freedom of conscience, and the prudence never to use them'.

A very similar trajectory was followed in the other two sets of decisions that related to the rights of communists. Great difficulties had been caused for communist defendants by the intimidation of counsel and potential counsel through the contempt citations upheld against two of the Dennis attorneys and the spread of loyalty oaths amongst many state Bar Associations. In the mid-1950s, things appeared to be improving when the Court quashed the citations of the Dennis lawyers and declared that past party membership was not proof of 'bad character'. But in a couple of 1961 cases, *Konigsberg* v. *State of California* and *In re George Anastaplo*, the Court maintained that whilst party membership might not be sufficient ground for exclusion from the bar, refusal to answer questions on this point was. The irony of the *Anastaplo* case was that Mr Anastaplo had become a staunch anti-communist who believed in the strict construction of the Bill of Rights (Auerbach, 1976, pp. 241–6, 249–53).

A similar reluctance to give up its capacity to manage freedom of expression was evidenced by the Court in its decisions relating to the legality of Congressional Investigations such as those of HUAC. In *Watkins* v. *United States* (1961), the Court appeared to have strictly curtailed these investigations through its insistence that according to the Constitution they were not permissible unless they possessed 'legislative purpose'. But in a series of decisions, culminating in *Wilkinson* v. *United States* (1961), the Court retreated from this position through, on Martin Shapiro's analysis, invoking the 'presumption doctrine' that Congressional investigations have legislative intent just because they are Congressional investigations (Shapiro, 1964, pp. 63–7).

The history of the litigation in the Communist Party cases demonstrates very clearly the limited influence of 'preferred position' theory as a means for safeguarding individual rights. Here, where virtually no plausible, let alone provable, threat to the social order seemed likely to follow from the granting to communists of the full freedoms of speech etc., these were at first totally denied, then partially restored on technicalities, and finally restricted again on technicalities. Given that African-Americans, defendants in criminal trials, trade unionists, and, later, pornographers and purveyors of 'hate speech', as well as women and sexual minorities all did better by the Supreme Court than the tiny Communist Party, it seems clear that the Court 'realistically' gave only that amount of freedom that the particular petitioner's social power indicated was prudent, and that it sought to confine the content of 'free' speech within particular bounds, because of the pressures in a situation where anti-communism had become equated with patriotism.

All in all, this added up to a significant change in the nature of the law as a mode of liberal governance; that is, to what Miller has called its 'politicisation': 'Law has increasingly become a purposive tool for the furtherance of desired goals rather than a set of interdictory commands limiting the discretion of administrators or canalising their decisions' (Miller, 1968, p. 107). Referring to the same development but connecting it with the theme of individuality, Theodore Lowi (1969, p. 144) similarly concluded:

> modern law has become a series of instructions to administrators rather than a series of commands to citizens. If at the same time (1) public control has become more positive, issuing imperatives along with setting limits, and if at the same time (2) application of laws has become more discretionary, by virtue of having become more indirect as well as more abstract, why should we assume we are talking about the same governmental phenomena in 1968 as in 1938 or 1908? The citizen has become an administré, the question now is how to be certain he remains a citizen?

Looking back, one can see that the Supreme Court during the period 1955–65 redefined 'the rule of law' so that the individual subject might more purposefully and effectively govern his or her affairs and in so doing define themselves as loyal citizens. In the short term, this effort was successful. Aggrieved citizens like African-Americans, the elderly and the very poor in need of health care, and trade union members appear to have accepted the rights offered as promising to improve the substantiveness of their freedom even as they protested that they were either insufficient or misconceived. Trade unions started to do something about their own discriminatory practices, whilst civil rights supporters evolved a strategy of non-violent civil disobedience that indicated acceptance of the principle of legal regulation, albeit in the breach. By contrast, other aggrieved citizens, like communists and southern racists, either lacked any meaningful public support for their rejectionism or in the latter case failed to gain majority backing for their 'massive resistance' (Murphy, 1962).

Thus, the 'balancing test' that the Warren Court often suggested it was applying was not simply one between legal categories such as First Amendment liberties and governmental powers, but also one between social interests. The effective imposition of the test was confirmation of the regulatory power of the law. More specifically, the Warren Court's major achievements were twofold: it made it easier for individuals to stand on their own two feet when faced with situations such as criminal prosecutions, unanticipated injuries, unfair contracts, and racism; and it established rather strict limits to legitimate dissent.

Because of the internal developments outlined above and a plethora of statutory measures, and despite the multiplying, code-like 'Restatements', the common law and its component discourses became subject to a process of disintegration – 'the collapse of contract into tort' (Gilmore, 1974), 'the disintegration of property' (Grey, 1980) and the qualifications to the universality of the negligence principle in torts (White, 1980). As a consequence, the common law could no longer be turned to as an authoritative source of guidance, at least not as the only such source, the *Restatements* notwithstanding. However, this did not mean that the great legal signs and the rights that define them disappeared from the law. On the contrary, they were and remain very much present, but *within* statutorily defined and codified discourses, facilitating their articulation, rather than *without*, defining principles and rules. In Realist terms, property, contract and tort represent the concepts with which lawyers are trained to think, to which they turn in moments of difficulty, and in terms of which their textbooks are differentiated and internally organised. Moreover, as statutes entered what Gilmore (1977, p. 96) called their 'middle age' and in the absence of either the political will or the support necessary to renew or replace them, the importance of the great signs and their associated bundles of rights increased once again as 'new issues, which no one ever dreamed of, present[ed] themselves for decision'. In such circumstances 'courts . . . may take matters in their own hands and do whatever justice and good sense may require'. As Guido Calabresi (1982, p. 165) put it, in an age of 'statutorification', judicial reform was the only means of maintaining the vitality of the law in the face of 'technological, societal, and even ideological changes'. Some prescient scholars writing in the 1970s even suggested that the resulting revival of common law reasoning might, or even should, usher in a new era of abstract conceptualism (Summers, 1969; White, 1980; MacNeil, 1980).

CONCLUSION

By 1977, the political managers of the American state, of whatever party, appear to have both lost faith in 'politicised' law and decided that they could no longer live up to their social modernist ideals. Four years earlier, confronted with spiralling inflation, a growing budget deficit, falling corporate profits, Opec's dramatic oil price rises, and continuing social disaffection and disorder, the Nixon Administration had decided that the best solution was to cut the already minimal help offered to the poor and so renege on the promise of equal opportunities for all (Woodiwiss, 1993, ch 7). President Nixon, of course, had to step down from the presidency, not because of anything he had done to the poor but for trying to cover up something he had done to an alternative set of political managers, the leaders of the Democratic Party. In his inaugural speech of 1977, Nixon's elected successor, Jimmy Carter, tried to restore the moral reputation of the Presidency and the country, but not by remembering the promise of equal opportunities, let alone by restoring the programmes that Nixon had cut. Instead he declared human rights to be the 'soul' of the United States government's foreign policy (Sellars, 2002, ch. 6; see also, Chandler, 2002, on the diffusion of the idea of an 'ethical foreign policy'). Human rights has retained this honorific position ever since, hence the Helsinki Accords, the conditions attached to American aid and trade agreements, and the State Department's annual reports on the human rights records of other states.

In the present context, I would like to put to one side the obvious questions as to the meaning, accuracy and advisability of the claimed possession of such a 'soul' in the light of, respectively, the continuing abuse of the rights of African-Americans, the narrowness of the American understanding of human rights, successive Administrations' selectivity in applying even American human rights standards, and the inherent unlikeliness of the idea of a moral superpower. Instead, I would simply like to point out that it represents disturbing evidence as to the continuing vitality of the human rights paradox, in that, whatever benefits America's human rights diplomacy may or may not have brought to the rest of the world, it presaged a dramatic increase in inequality both in the United States itself (Phillips, 1990; Woodiwiss, 1993, ch.8), and the rest of the world. The key legal development linking or subverting, depending on one's point of view, the rise of human rights diplomacy with increased domestic and global inequality was the creation of an extremely powerful counter-discourse to the anyway already subordinated elements inspired by the principle of reciprocity within human rights discourse as it developed within the context of the UN.

This counter-discourse was, of course, that which became popularly known as Reaganism or neo-liberalism. Within legal theory, Friedrich von Hayek's long established fascination with the interrelationships between law and economics was one of the main inspirations for a new formalism in the form of the school of thought known as 'Law and Economics', which rapidly triumphed over a marxisant neo-Realism that became known as Critical Legal Studies in a battle for influence over mainstream legal scholarship. The two leading representatives of the Law and Economics School are Ronald Coase and Richard Posner. To speak of just one of them and putting it simply, Coase's solution to the problem posed by the increasing incoherence of the law was that the law should refound itself on the basis of an updated version of laissez-faire economics since the combination of clear property rights and free competition leads to the optimum use of resources and optimal solutions to problems. What makes this idea an 'updated' version of laissez-faire are two things. First, for Coase, the market can only work properly if everything in the world, including the air we breathe, is privately owned and therefore can be brought to, or 'internalised' within, the market. As long as anything remains un-owned, it must be regarded as an 'externality', which either has to be paid for if it is damaged, or, worse, has to be entrusted to the state which will levy taxes in order to protect it. Second, remodelling the law on the market will greatly reduce the extent and cost of the law. For Coase, where things remain un-owned, it is very difficult to decide who should pay if they are damaged, hence the extent and ever increasing complexity and 'transaction costs' of the law as different solutions are tried and fail. It is a mark of the seriousness and depth of this still ongoing effort to ensure the continuing exclusion of the principle of reciprocity from rights discourse that it soon included its own historical reworking of Dicey's understanding of the relationship between rights and capitalism in the form of John W. Ely's *The Guardian of Every Other Liberty: a Constitutional History of Property Rights* (1992). In the following chapter, I will return to the story of human rights in the UN where the parallels with the American story as regards the constraining of reciprocity and the resulting 'marketisation' (Baxi, 2002, ch. 5) of human rights represent a striking demonstration of American power.

9

THE UNITED NATIONS AND THE INTERNATIONALISATION OF AMERICAN RIGHTS DISCOURSE

Returning to developments within the UN, the absence of a right to property from either of the two principal covenants, the judgmental reticence and drafting activities of the Human Rights Commission, plus the Commision's promulgation of the doctrine of the indivisibility of the two covenants, all suggested that the possibility of the discourse refounding itself on a more clearly cosmopolitan or chthonic basis was not altogether closed off.[1] Moreover, by 1971 the UN was a very different body from what it had been at its inception. In addition to the original 58, decolonisation had produced many new members. Also, because of its globally unpopular involvement in Vietnam, the United States no longer held the moral high ground, particularly in the eyes of the state-socialist and postcolonial states. Further, the economic and political challenges of the 1960s had reinforced the commitment of many Western-European states, including Britain, to corporatist social policies that emphasised economic and social claims rooted in the principle of reciprocity, at the same time as their social-democratic parties retreated from any commitment to socialism as even their ultimate goal. Finally, not only were the former Axis Powers, Japan and West Germany, now members of the UN but both were clearly on their way to becoming not only major economic powers but also strong supporters of communitarian over individualistic ideas. In sum, the Soviet Union and its eastern European allies, thanks to these developments, their own very erratic reform efforts and their on/off alliance with China, were no longer either so socially distinctive, so friendless, or so easily anathematised.

As this rather different institutional and global setting had developed, new state and non-state actors claimed a say in defining the nature of human rights. As a consequence, social, economic and cultural rights secured their place within human rights discourse, albeit an inferior one when compared with civil and political rights. Thus the two Covenants were not only completed but also in 1966, after a long delay caused by the initial intensity of the cold war (Evans, 1996; Sellars, 2002, ch. 4), submitted for approval by the General Assembly and subsequent ratification by member states. They came into force once the requisite number of ratifications had been obtained, which was in 1976. In Steiner and Alston's (1996: 126) concise summary and in addition to the right of national self-determination, the rights contained within the ICCPR and rooted in the principle of autonomy are:

1 protection of the individual's physical integrity, as in provisions on torture, arbitrary arrest, arbitrary deprivation of life;
2 procedural fairness when government deprives an individual of liberty, as in provisions on arrest, trial procedure and conditions of imprisonment;
3 equal protection norms defined in religious, gender and other terms;
4 freedoms of belief, speech and association, such as provisions on the practice of religion, press freedom and the right to hold assembly and form associations; and
5 the right to political participation.

Likewise, the central provisions of the ICESCR which are rooted in the principle of reciprocity may be briefly summarised as:

1 the right to national self-determination (again);
2 the rights to work, just and favourable conditions at work and the right to form and join trade unions;
3 the rights to social security, family and mother/child support and protection in childhood;
4 the rights to an adequate standard of living, physical and mental health and education;
5 the rights to cultural participation, knowledge and copyright;

6 equal protection norms defined in religious, gender, racial and other terms.

In this way the doctrine of the indivisibility of the two sets of rights, which had been developed earlier to reduce the divisive consequences of the drawing up of two separate covenants, gained substance, not only because detailed specification of the two sets of rights made it easier to see that they at least overlapped, but also because a practical, rather than principled, rationale was agreed for their continuing separation, namely the distinction between 'justiciable' civil and political rights and 'programmatic' economic and social rights. This distinction was made explicit in the official annotations to the draft texts of the two covenants:

> Those in favour of drafting two separate covenants argued that *civil and political rights were enforceable, or justiciable, or of an absolute character, while economic, social and cultural rights were not or might not be; that the former were immediately applicable, while the latter were to be progressively implemented*; and that, generally speaking, the former were rights of the individual against the state . . . while the latter were rights which the state would have to take positive action to promote . . . The question of drafting one or two covenants was intimately related to the question of implementation . . . Since the rights could be divided into two broad categories, which should be subject to different procedures of implementation, it would be both logical and convenient to formulate two separate covenants.
> (quoted in Steiner and Alston, 1996: 261, emphasis added)

This move in the direction of consensus, albeit still on the western-defined basis of the privileging of civil and political over economic and social rights, was accompanied by a similarly explainable move in the direction of more active modes of interrogation of the membership's behaviour as regards the human rights of their citizens – the UN now listened far more attentively, and it began to question and look. This process had begun in 1959 when ECOSOC (Resolution 28) repeated its invitation to the citizens of member states to communicate any complaints to the Secretary General. In 1967 ECOSOC (Resolution 1235) sanctioned a decision by the Human Rights Commission to engage in an annual public debate on any gross violations known to it and also, if necessary, to engage in thorough studies of such violations with a view to making recommendations both to the state concerned and, again if necessary, to one or other of the UN organs for further action.

Three years later, in 1970, ECOSOC (Resolution 1503) authorised its Sub-Commission on the Prevention of Discrimination and Protection of Minorities to consider complaints concerning gross violations and any governmental responses already received under conditions of confidentiality and with a view to ascertaining whether or not they indeed revealed a consistent pattern of gross and reliably attested violations of human rights ... within [its] terms of reference (quoted in Steiner and Alston, 1996: 376). In cases where the Sub-Commission feels there is cause for concern, it is empowered to refer them to the Commission on Human Rights for detailed study with a view to the Commission making recommendations to other UN organs, again under conditions of confidentiality unless it decides to transfer the issue to the public 1235 procedure.

Finally, a state's ratification of either or both of the general covenants means that, according to international law, and as signatories of treaties rather than simply the supporters of a declaration, they incur binding legal obligations in respect of the content of the covenants. The first of these obligations is the quinquennial filing of reports on implementation with the Human Rights Committee created by the ICCPR – a committee whose members were initially, and largely remain, lawyers – and the far more tardily formed Committee on Economic, Social and Cultural Rights. These reports are then considered by the relevant committee which returns them with its own comments, criticisms and requests for further information or supplementary reports in the hope of stimulating improved performance. Signatories to the First Optional Protocol to the ICCPR, which allows their citizens to make direct complaints to the Committee, also incur the obligation to at least receive the Committees views of the complaint. All of these requirements and procedures also apply to signatories to the Convention on the Elimination of Racial Discrimination (CERD), which was approved by the General Assembly in 1965 and came into force in 1969.

As well as the legal expertise located in the Human Rights Committee, legal concepts and ways of thinking gradually displaced political ones in the UN's handling of human rights issues (Rancharan, 1997). This is particularly clear in the way that the Committee made, and was allowed to make, international law through its General Comments, which address not simply procedural issues associated with the improvement of the quality of the reports they receive but also bear on issues of interpretation with respect to the meanings of articles and the criteria for proper implementation. Also, the investigations and reports or views under Resolutions 1235 and 1503, as well as the responses to individual complaints allowed by the First Optional Protocol, took on an increasingly judicial cast. The net result was that much of the activity undertaken during the 1970s may be summarised as the transcribing of politically inspired texts into legal language. Thus, and at least in relation to the older covenants, legal modes of reasoning and principles became the chief strategic resource defining the future direction of the human rights project. As a result, not only was Socialism if not Liberalism displaced as such a resource, but also the issue of the relationship between political ideology and human rights was pushed further and further into the background. This, like the earlier exclusion of the right to private property from the Covenants, latterly proved to be politically advantageous to the United States as the détente between the superpowers developed. That is, the social-structural differences implicit in divergent political ideologies tended to disappear from human rights discourse as in any way pertinent to the issue of enforcement. Moreover, the fact that they disappeared in a largely capitalist world, whether measured numerically or in terms of the distribution of economic resources, and that the medium through which they disappeared was that of liberal western law, meant that economic and social rights and therefore the principle of reciprocity from which they are derived were further marginalised.

THE JURIDIFICATION OF HUMAN RIGHTS DISCOURSE

By1990, the human rights project was in a state of some crisis. The weakening and eventual collapse of the Soviet Union had allowed tensions between the Republican and cosmopolitan readings of human rights that had been suppressed by the realpolitik of the cold war to come to the surface in the form of a strong reassertion by some states of the pertinence of, and the challenges posed by, social-structural and cultural differences. The source of this crisis was the tension created by the simultaneous occurrence of three developments that affected the play of forces within the UN system: the increased influence of largely western-based NGOs committed to enlarging and deepening the ambit of human rights discourse; the rise of neo-liberalism in the United States and Britain in particular; and the increased cultural assertiveness of many Asian states as some insisted on their Islamic culture and others drew confidence from their economic achievements, including China, which became more engaged in global and UN politics (Bauer and Bell, 1999; Davis, 1995; Langlois, 2001; Tang, 1995; Woodiwiss, 1998).

The NGOs were successful in that the 1979 Convention on the Elimination of all Forms of Discrimination against Women (CEDAW) became effective in 1981, the 1984 Convention against Torture (CAT) in 1985, and the 1989 Convention on the Rights of the Child (CRC) in 1990. However, the effect of these conventions was somewhat reduced by the simultaneous development of resistances on two fronts. The first was represented by some western nations rejecting any pressure on them to enhance economic and social rights, even if they were thought necessary to counter the effects of past discrimination on minorities, women or children. Not only did the Reagan and Bush Administrations continue to refuse to contemplate the ratification of the ICESCR, but they also suspended the ratification process of the ICCPR that the Carter Administration had initiated, and strongly resisted the very idea of the possibility of such 'third generation' or 'group rights' as those of indigenous peoples, as well as rights to development and communication (see below, pp. 124–5). The second was that represented by some Asian states' equally strong rejection of any insistence on the enhancement of civil and political rights. In the first case, resistance was justified by the economic success of an unshackled capitalism and the political victory of liberal democracy over socialism. In the second, most powerfully expressed in the 1993 Bangkok Government Declaration which preceded the UN's Second World Conference on Human Rights held later the same year in Vienna, untrammelled liberal democracy was seen as an obstacle to the achievement of the same economic success and therefore to the advancement of economic and social rights. Also, certain aspects of the project to enhance women's rights in particular were regarded as culturally imperialistic.

In the meantime, the interrogation of the human rights records of the signatories to the growing number of covenants, signatories which in 1990 still did not include the United States and China, had become even more detailed and insistent consequent not only on the steadily improving administrative and legal rigour of the procedures involved but also on the increased access granted to NGOs – by 1994, 900 NGOs had official consultative status with the UN, whilst 1,500 were represented at the Vienna Conference. Thus, not only did the Committees set up under the various conventions become more demanding and critical with respect to the content of the reports that had to be filed with them, but the number of complaints they received grew exponentially – until the mid-1980s the UN received, on average, 25,000 complaints per year. Ten years later this number had ballooned to around 300,000, but many of these complaints are identical as a result of letter-writing campaigns by groups with a large and active membership (Steiner and Alston, 1996: 380). Moreover, not only was the appointment of rapporteurs empowered to make site visits added to the range of methods of fact-finding available to the committees, but also 'thematic mechanisms' were instituted by the Commission, which provide for the continuing monitoring of areas of concern by either working groups or special rapporteurs. In 1995, 13 such mechanisms were in operation. They were concerned with: disappearances, arbitrary detention, extra-judicial executions, freedom of expression, racial discrimination, torture, religious intolerance, use of mercenaries, commercial sexual abuse of children, internally displaced persons, judicial independence, violence against women and the effects of toxic and dangerous products on human rights.

In this context, the various UN human rights committees became ever more confidently judicial in their reasoning and the tone of their comments and views (McGoldrick, 1991). Thus, and, as it has turned out, fatefully, even the once-formidable barrier to the jurisdiction of the UN's human rights institutions represented by national sovereignty was overcome, legally at least, as Louis Sohn (1995) and Steiner and Alston (1996: 369–72) have shown in their accounts of the UN's relations with the previous regimes in South Africa and Poland respectively (see also, Mills, 1998). This development was buttressed by the emergence of regional human rights jurisdictions in the forms of the European Court of Human Rights, the African Commission on Human and Peoples' Rights, and the Inter-American Court for Human Rights.

However, the UN is by no means coextensive with global law and developments outside the ambit of the UN have had a largely unnoticed and, in my judgement, negative significance for the present and future of human rights. Just as neo-liberalism has provided much of the rationale for economic globalisation, so Law and Economics has provided much of the rationale behind a 'new [global] constitutionalism' (Gill, 1995 cited by Schneiderman, 2000). As David Schneiderman writes, summarising Steven Gill:

> The new constitutionalism refers to the quasi-legal restructuring of the state and the institutionalisation of international political forms that emphasise market credibility and efficiency and also limit the the processes of democratic decision making within nation states. The project mandates the insulation of key aspects of the economy from the influence of politicians or the mass of citizens 'by imposing, internally and externally, "binding constraints" on the conduct of fiscal, monetary, trade, and investment policies' (Gill, 1995, p. 412). By limiting state action with regard to key aspects of economic life, the new constitutionalism confers privileged rights of citizenship and representation on corporate capital, while at the same time constraining democratic processes. Central to the new constitutionalism, then, is the imposition

of 'discipline' on state institutions, both 'to prevent national interference with property rights and [to provide] entry and exit options for holders of mobile capital with regard to particular political jurisdictions'.

(Schneiderman, 2000, p. 758; Gill, 1995, p. 413)

Thus, as exemplified by the rules of the World Trade Organisation (WTO), the World Bank, the IMF and the United States' currently burgeoning number of bilateral free trade agreements, the sanctity of property rights has been embedded at the core of international economic law and regulation (Qureshi, 1999; Likosky, 2002). Although the right to private property disappeared from international human rights discourse between the adoption of the UDHR, where it was present, and the completion of the texts of the ICCPR and the ICESCR in 1954, from which it was absent, by the 1990s property right had once again been restored to its former position of primacy within rights discourse, and not just in the United States but globally.

CONCLUSION

In sum, then, the continuing influence of the United States and its allies amongst other developed northern states on the development of international human rights discourse is clearly apparent in the way in which international rights discourse has developed in parallel with American developments. On the one hand, several of the more civil-libertarian initiatives promoted by western-led NGOs with respect to the prohibition of torture and the rights of racial or ethnic minorities, women and children have been incorporated into the international discourse. On the other hand, the American-led group has thus far successfully used the doctrine of justiciability, recently reinforced by the 'new [global] constitutionalism', to resist initiatives promoted by, in turn, the communist, southern, indigenous and Asian states and/or NGOs on behalf of economic, social and cultural rights, indigenous rights and the rights to development, information and communication. In sum, where the threat to property rights has been small, initiatives have been successful, whilst, where the threat to property rights has been substantial, initiatives have been blocked. This said, the challenges to the sanctity of property right and the alternative vision of a more chthonic and cosmopolitan human rights discourse have both become much more substantial globally than in the United States itself. Ironically from an American perspective, this is largely because of the global diffusion of civil and political rights which, where it has been successful, has led not to the multiplication of simulacra of

American rights discourse but to the revivification of more communitarian traditions. That is, as in the case of formalism in the early part of the twentieth century, an expertise and a technique of governance developed in the hope of one effect has turned out to have facilitated another. Although Japan's post-war geopolitical subordination to the United States meant that it did not lead or even often support the aforementioned challenges, the Japanese rights culture is very much a case in point.

10

MAKING AN EXAMPLE OF JAPAN

Japan's defeat in the Pacific War ushered in a period of very rapid social change in that country. As in the United States in the 1930s, political change preceded and produced socio-economic and legal changes. Until 1952, Japan was occupied by the Allies under the very assertive leadership of the United States and the Supreme Commander, General MacArthur. However, in a manner that turned out to prefigure accurately the eventual significance of the reforms that accompanied the Occupation, Japan was deprived of her sovereignty for the Occupation's duration and yet continued to rule herself. The Occupation authorities or SCAP (Supreme Commander Allied Powers) initiated or approved all the major pieces of legislation, including the 'New Constitution' (Quigley and Turner, 1956; Ward, 1957), the reform of the legal Codes and the legal system more generally, the legalisation of trade unions (Gould, 1984, ch.1), the dismemberment of the huge pre-war corporations or *zaibatsu,* and a very radical programme of land reform. However, and despite the fact that this legislative package represented a bold attempt at social engineering or nation building, as it would be called today, all items in the package were debated and passed by the Diet, promulgated by the Emperor, implemented by the state bureaucracy, administered by the courts and enforced by the Japanese authorities. Moreover, until 1947, all of these institutions continued to operate more or less as they had done under the pre-war regime and mainly with the same personnel.

Perhaps for this reason and despite the initial hostility of the Japanese Communist Party and some continuing reservations on the part of the political right, the Occupation reforms were accommodated by Japanese society, which changed in some ways but was by no means totally transformed (cp. Ramlogan, 1994). The constitutional changes were considered by the Diet as if they were simply a series of amendments to the Meiji Constitution. Most subsequent scholarly comment has considered this to have been a subterfuge forced upon the Diet by Occupation authorities anxious to find a way around the commitment made as part of the Potsdam Declaration of 1945 that the Japanese people should be free to choose their own post-war constitution. Whether or not any anxiety existed as to how the Japanese might use any such freedom (that is, socialistically), and there certainly seem to be grounds for thinking that it did (Ward, 1957, p. 648), the answer to the question as to how the constitutional changes that were made may most accurately be described is, I think, less obvious than is generally supposed. In other words, the text of the New Constitution may still be read as signifying something of what was signified by the Meiji Constitution. And this despite the following: the claims to democratism explicitly made in the preamble; the insertion of a new Chapter II (the 'peace clause'); the deletion of many provisions that had been restrictive of individual liberty; the addition of several explicitly liberal-democratic liberties and claims; and, finally, the supremacy of an elected Diet over the executive.

The preamble was ostensibly written from the point of view of a sovereign people supposedly anxious to enjoy the very Christian- and American-sounding 'blessings of liberty'. And yet the order in which they 'chose' to set out the basis upon which they proposed to pursue such enjoyment was to all intents and purposes the same as that earlier determined by the Emperor. The significance of this is that Chapter I still defines the position and powers of the Emperor and would still have been followed by a listing of 'the rights and duties of the people', were it not for the rather clumsily inserted 'peace clause', whose presence at this point makes the Occupation's arm-twisting palpable. The Emperor's position is defined as that of 'the symbol of the State and of the unity of the people, deriving his position from the will of the people, with whom resides sovereign power'. However, the discursive ordering of the document may be read as undermining this somewhat by prompting a series of questions: should not the nature and the rights of the sovereign (i.e. 'the people') have been specified before those of their 'symbol'? Can a sovereign *qua* sovereign have duties imposed upon it and if so who or what could impose them and would not he, she or it in fact be the sovereign?

In response to the first question a positive answer seems called for, since otherwise, as with the Meiji Constitution, it appears that rights are granted by, and that duties are owed to, the Emperor. This said, and responding to the second question, there need be no conflict between what we know the 'New Constitution' was intended to say about the location of sovereignty and what its ordering might suggest, provided that the identity of the sovereign is not in doubt. The idea that the people as sovereign may impose duties upon themselves as subjects – that is, the idea of the social contract – is of course basic to liberal-democratic political philosophy and, therefore, if the sovereign and the people are unambiguously one and the same there is no problem. This is not the case in the New Constitution. The Emperor is not defined simply as 'the symbol of the people' but as 'the symbol of the State *and* of the unity of the people' (emphasis added). According to liberal-democratic thought, the state is the unity of the people. Thus to distinguish the two concepts, as is done in the New Constitution and as is emphasised by the use of the capital 'S' in 'State', suggests that a basic law that may be read in other than liberal-democratic ways was promulgated in the New Constitution. Specifically, it suggests: a) that the state is distinguishable from and is in some sense co-sovereign with the people; b) that, therefore, it too can grant rights and impose duties in its own interest; and c) that the traditional distinction between the state and 'the great treasure' was still operative, albeit in a somewhat qualified way. This, then, is the source of the ambiguity that makes it possible that the New Constitution might still signify something of what the Meiji Constitution signified by way of the superiority of the state vis-à-vis the citizenry.

That the government and some Diet members, at least, were aware of this ambiguity and its latent ideological significance is clear from the following summary of part of the House of Representatives' debate on the Constitution:

> By far the most absorbing questions were those of the meaning and future locus of sovereignty, which were closely entwined with others relating to the national structure and the position of the dynasty. Hara Fujiro, Shimpoto, invited Mr. Kanamori [the minister responsible, A.W.] to disentangle from one another the conceptions that sovereignty resided in the state, that it belonged to the people, and that the Emperor was a participant in sovereignty as one of the people. Kanamori responded that 'if the word 'sovereignty' is to be taken as the source from which the will of the state is actually derived . . . I think it right to answer that in Japan 'sovereignty', without any doubt, resides in the

whole people, including the Emperor.' He continued: 'Mr. Hara wanted to know in what part of the draft Constitution, then, that connotation was provided for. That is not written in so many words in the draft Constitution. That is because in Japan the Emperor and the people are one, the whole people being bound together through the spiritual ties with the Emperor which are deep-rooted in the bottom of their hearts, and this union constitutes the foundation of the existence of the state. This fact requires no explanation'.

(Quigley and Turner, 1956, p. 133; see also pp. 151 ff.)

As it has turned out, the ambiguity as to the location of sovereignty and the sense of historical continuity that this has preserved have provided the principal bases upon which it has proved possible to establish a secularised and reconstructed form of imperial patriarchalism in the context of the rule of law: 'secularised' because the Emperor repudiated his 'divinity' in the Imperial Rescript of 1 January 1946; 'reconstructed' because it has had to accommodate the changes forced by the democratisation that the Occupation set in train.

Thus Japan's discourse of rule was sociologised as well as secularised by the somewhat ambiguous transfer of sovereignty from the Emperor to the people in that the central role as the embodiment of Japan's uniqueness, hitherto played by the Emperor was taken by the *ie* (the traditional extended patriarchalist family). In other words, the uniqueness of their society, which only some of the communists and socialists doubted, gradually came to be seen by most Japanese as lying in their special 'way of life'. Thus the society appears to have experienced what might be called a 'Durkheimian revelation' concerning the relation between the sacred and the social, except that for Durkheim (1976) the discovery that in worshipping its gods a society was in fact worshipping itself destroyed the basis for religious belief as such. In post-war Japan this does not seem to have been the result. The veneration once reserved for the ancestral spirits and the Emperor and the duties consequently owed to them was in large part transferred to such institutions as the *ie* or, more substantively following the legal demise of the *ie* (see below), to the institutions and especially the *kaisha* (large companies) which supposedly embody the *ie* essence today. Hence the name I and others have given to Japan's post-war discourse of rule: *Kigyoushugi* (belief in the intrinsic virtue of the company) (Woodiwiss, 1993, pp. 85–91).

The continuities represented by the continuing importance of patriarchalism or familialism between pre- and post-war constitutional arrangements and their associated discourses of rule had rather striking consequences for the way in which Japan's imported rights discourse developed. The Occupation's immediate repeal of all the most outrageously repressive laws, including the Peace Preservation Act, its reining-in and reform of the police and its grant of the franchise to women, were all followed up in the Constitution by the promulgation of rights to the classical liberal freedoms, which were extended to include the 'right of workers to organize and to bargain and act collectively', and to some 'social rights': e.g. to 'minimum standards of wholesome and cultured living', to 'the promotion and extension of social welfare and security, and of public health', to an 'equal education correspondent to their ability'.

Significant though the enhancements of freedom and the support for democratic values consequent upon the promulgation of these rights undoubtedly were and are, it is nevertheless necessary to point out that the chapter wherein they are set down contains its own echoes of the Meiji Constitution. These echoes include: the provisions of Chapter III which insist in one way or another that, in the words of Article 12, 'the people shall refrain from any abuse of these freedoms . . . and shall always be responsible for utilising them for the public welfare'. In contrast to the Meiji Constitution, the possibility of restrictions on these freedoms and rights is not stated directly, except in relation to property right and, strangely, the freedom of abode and occupation. Rather it is present in the interpretive convention which requires all Articles to be read in the light of one another. When made explicit and articulated with the traditional imperial themes latent within Chapter I, these echoes have in fact turned out to have had restrictive consequences not only for the actual extent of democratic freedoms but also, as the American sociologist David Riesman pointed out, for the very meaning of the term 'democracy':

> One has to take care that one does not misinterpret what the Japanese mean by 'democracy', a word they constantly use. It does not mean social equality: the consideration, for example, shown one's equals and official superiors is not extended to those below. 'Democracy' does seem to mean a way of doing business that combines commitment and high principle with lack of factionalism and internecine conflict. People refer to organizations as 'undemocratic' if there is no harmony or consensus. Thus democracy and politics would seem antithetical.
>
> (quoted in Nakane, 1970, pp. 148 ff.)

A case in point as regards the indirectly imposed restrictions of concern here, is that relating to the state's responsibilities for 'the public welfare'. Here the restrictive potential anyway and anywhere implicit in the idea of 'the public welfare', and which always coexists with its more often acknowledged expansive potential, was greatly enhanced by Article 27, which states that 'All people shall have the right and the *obligation* to work' (emphasis added). However, in contrast to the Meiji Constitution, the occasion for any actual restriction may no longer be the mere existence of law allowing it, since such a law must itself pass 'the public welfare' test. And this test is administered by a Supreme Court which, thanks to Article 81 and its grant of the power of judicial review, is now the guardian of the Constitution. For example, the ultimate justification for any restrictions on freedoms or rights can no longer be simply the respect due to the Emperor-state but must be instead a secular rationale, which must take into account such freedoms and rights as the Constitution grants. That this rationale, as it has evolved, has gained an increasingly conservative inflexion, despite or perhaps because of the Court's reluctance to use its power of judicial review (see below), is the consequence of the Liberal Democratic Party's successes in post-war electoral contests, as well as of the not unrelated continuing power of the state bureaucracy. To put the point another way, what the courts might have come to regard as 'the public welfare' would in all likelihood have been very different had the Japan Socialist Party (JSP) also held power for any length of time.

As was indicated earlier, personal and private rights in general were greatly strengthened by the Occupation reforms with the ostensible exception of those of private property-holders. In addition, individuals acquired rights of redress against the state through administrative courts. The autonomy of the judiciary was considerably enhanced thanks to the Supreme Court's gaining of the power, if requested by the citizenry, to review government actions and legislation with a view to establishing their constitutionality. The judiciary's position was also strengthened by its gaining of the power to impose the sanctions of the criminal law (for contempt of court) on its own behalf, although this power remains very underdeveloped as compared to that available in common law societies (Haley, 1982a). Finally, as if to symbolise the potential significance of both these and the accompanying extralegal developments, the *koseki* (registers) that were formerly central to the system of social control were restructured on the basis of the nuclear rather than the extended family.

By depriving the *ie*, both institutionally and ideologically, of its critical role as the intermediary institution between the individual and the state, the restructuring of the registers struck at the heart of the old imperial way. This was an attack continued by the two-stage reform of the Civil Code which occurred in 1947 and 1948, and whose principal concern was the reform of family relationships. As a result of the changes to the

Code, primogeniture was abolished, wives gained control over their own property, mothers gained equality with fathers with respect to matters concerning children, women gained the same divorce rights as men and in numerous other ways the bases were created for a more egalitarian family structure and, by extension, a more individualised citizenry.

To create a basis for something does not, of course, ensure that the desired state of affairs will come about. And certainly, neither the democratisation of the Japanese family nor that of the relations between men and women more generally followed automatically from the introduction of these reforms. The same may be said of social relations more generally. As has already been mentioned, individual rights are still subject to a 'public welfare' test, which has meant that because of the invention of new duties they are more restricted than they need be. However, it should also be said that the general trend in decisions involving this test has been one of liberalisation (Beer, 1984, ch. 12; Oda, 2000, ch. 6; Krotoszynski, 1998). This said, in the present context it is particularly important to point out, following Beer (1968), that the manner in which this has been achieved has typically been by 'harmonising' (that is, hierarchising) conflicting positions rather than by balancing them in the American manner (see above, p. 99). The judiciary is still very loath to exercise its powers of review and redress in relation to the acts and activities of the state (Hamano, 1999). However, this is not necessarily a bad thing in a democracy, where the governing party may be reasonably presumed to have a mandate from a majority of the population (Haley, 1986). Here again, for good or ill, the evidence suggests that this inhibition has become somewhat less marked than it was, especially in the lower courts (Ishimine, 1974; Ramlogan, 1994, p. 149–50).

As in most other advanced capitalist societies, the 'public interest' test gained a general pertinence to the degree that it provided the basis for adjudication in the absence of clear guidance from statutes and codes and/or case law. Indeed in civil law countries such as Japan its prominence in this role may sometimes be particularly marked, since judges and justices are less constrained by precedent. As in other societies, the prominence of a 'public interest' test carries the possibility that, in the absence of a clear, countervailing principle such as might be represented by the privileging of the rights of labour or of private property, judgments will depend upon the nature of the prevailing values and/or individual judges' understandings of them, as seems to be recognised to varying degrees by Japanese jurists (Itoh, 1970, pp. 785–804). What seems not to have been recognised by them, however, is that this possibility might also carry dangers, especially when the harmonising of rights is preferred to their balancing.

In a society where the state continues to possess a still unrivalled social pre-eminence, the degree of danger depends very much upon the degree of pluralism that these values exhibit and/or that judges are prepared to recognise in relation to the rights of citizens, as well as upon the maintenance of democratic accountability. A point whose importance should be well understood in Japan, given the pre-war experience of the 'judicial fascism' associated with the so-called 'free law' theory of Makino and his followers (Itoh, 1970, pp. 781–2).

In some contrast to the position adopted by scholars regarding its pre-war status (see above, p. 00), several students of post-war Japanese law have been critical of the constraints imposed upon property right (for example Ukai and Nathanson, 1968). Not only were such originally feudal forms of land holding as *emphyteusis* allowed to continue, but property rights, unlike 'life and liberty', were denied an American-style direct mention in Article 31, the 'due process' clause of the New Constitution. The fear, therefore, remains that the invocation of the 'public welfare' test might yet prove to be particularly deleterious to the rights of property-holders. This seems to me to be an exaggerated fear. First, because under democratic conditions and therefore in contrast to the conditions obtaining in the pre-war period, there is not the same danger that the public interest will be directly identified with that of the state. And, second, because as a matter of values and fact 'the public welfare' has been deemed in both the political and legal realms to include the protection and even the privileging of the rights of private property-holders.

Even before the LDP had established its post-war political dominance, this privilege was apparent in the law. The case in which it became explicit was the so-called 'production control case' of *Japan* v. *Okada* (1950) in which the Supreme Court ruled that the production control strikes (*seisan kanri*), which had been such a notable feature of early post-war industrial relations, were unconstitutional. This decision very definitely privileged the rights of capital relative to those of labour and hence there has been at the heart of post-war legal discourse a limit to the possible changes which might be wrought within that discourse so far as industrial relations are concerned.

This said, the gradual entry of *kigyoshugi* into labour law, for example, transformed the conception of the employment relationship in the private sector that was basic to both the New Constitution (1947) and the 1949 Trade Union Law. In other words, the post-war American-inspired recognition of the different interests of capital and labour that was fundamental to the Labour Law of 1949 of the period has been ever more confidently *denied* as the social and judicial commitment to the limited and hierarchical communitarianism of the company bespoken by *kigyoshugi* has grown. Consequently, the period since 1949 has seen, to use Hohfeld's language, the freedoms of Japanese employees and trade unions translated into not only an increase in powers (to participate in joint consultation fora, for example) and some very substantial increases in 'claims' to such as company welfare benefits and, most importantly, to an apparently irreversible claim to 'lifetime employment' – all justified by a familialist variant of reciprocity. In sum, these developments in Japanese labour law represent an instance of how the obligations inherent in the familialist (in this case Confucian) concept of 'benevolence' have been made legally enforceable thanks to the arrival of rights discourse and democracy and therefore instance a more general revivification of familialism (for accounts of the wider but less encouraging significance of this development in Asia and beyond, see Woodiwiss, 1998, 2003).

All in all, the net effect of the United States' imposition of a rights culture on Japan has been that, even when judged by western standards, Japan has by far the best human rights record in Asia. But, as has just been illustrated with respect to labour rights, this result has only been possible because of the creative way in which rights discourse has been articulated with the established familialist form of the principle of reciprocity and wider sets of social relations. This articulation, however, also explains some of the less impressive aspects of Japan's human rights record; that is, the relative weakness of the protections afforded those who either occupy subordinate statuses within the Japanese 'family', such as women, minorities, patients, children and those without strong communal ties (Goodman and Neary, 1996; Kim, 1998; Neary, 2002; Reber, 1999), or foreign workers (Hingwan, 1996).

CONCLUSION

Despite globalisation and because anyway globalisation cannot be reduced to Americanisation (see below, p. 144), the United States' increasingly narrow understanding of, and expertise in, human rights has not become *the* universal understanding of, nor exhausted the global stock of expertise in, human rights. There is no clearer confirmation of this fact than that represented by Japan's development of a variety of human rights discourse and associated modes of governance which are very different from America's in that reciprocity-based elements, albeit of a highly hierarchical nature, are far more important than the autonomy-based ones – and this despite having received 'the blessings of liberty' from the occupying power.

Thus, despite also the many particular and often forceful ways in which the United States has sought to influence the development of rights discourse in Japan since 1946, the net result has been to prompt a reinvention of Japanese patriarchalism or familialism and a competing conception of human rights which gives a much more important role to economic, social and cultural rights than they have been allowed to have in the United States. Indeed, the Japanese government has enthusiastically adopted the alternative to neo-liberalism first set out at the 1995 UN Social Summit in Copenhagen, and currently prefers to speak of 'human security' rather than human rights as the idea guiding its foreign and development policies:

> Each human being is equal in having its own potential. A person should be respected as an individual regardless of nationality, race, sex, etc. Human development has been promoted by the accumulation of creative activities by free individuals. However, it is extremely difficult for individuals to realise their potential and capabilities if their lives and livelihoods are threatened, and their dignity impaired. Under such conditions, the future of the whole society could be at stake as well as that of individual citizens.
>
> (The Trust Fund for Human Security, 2002, p. 1)

Japan, then, has been 'made an example of' with respect to human rights in three interlinked but quite different senses. First, rights discourse and democracy were forced upon Japan in order to punish its pre-war rulers for their aggression by preventing their revival. Second, as a consequence of the acceptance by the Japanese state and people of these impositions, Japan became the pre-eminently successful example of the beneficial effects that can follow from the embedding of respect for human rights within the social routines of non-western countries. Third, Japan has made an example of itself as the embodiment of a vision of human rights that, so far largely implicitly, represents a striking if quietly spoken challenge to the reigning American orthodoxy. In time, for good and ill, and especially if it is also taken up by China, this may prove to be a highly attractive alternative approach to human rights to many developing societies.

11

THE DESIRE FOR EQUALITY AND THE EMERGENCE OF A SOCIOLOGY *FOR* HUMAN RIGHTS

Although the United States and the West more generally have thus far been successful in constraining the effective meaning and the disciplinary power of international human rights within the narrow, 'market friendly' (Baxi, 2002, p. 132) limits defined by civil and political rights, this does not mean that there have not been serious challenges to these limits. Five of the most significant challenges have been on behalf of what I term the 'new universalism': a broader conception of personhood, so that protection is equally available irrespective of race, gender and sexuality; equal access to information and communications, so that all may enjoy freedom of expression; equal attention to all modes of social life in the development of human rights thought and practice, so that all may be equally protected no matter what kind of society they may live in – liberal, social-democratic, socialist, familialist, or whatever; equality of status for economic and social with civil and political rights, so that all may actually use and benefit from their rights; and both a right to development and respect for indigenous rights, so that the rich countries should meet their obligations to poor countries and threatened peoples.

The 'carnivalistic' (Baxi, 2002, p. 31) vigour with which the subaltern groups promoting these challenges have insisted on the presence of a reciprocal element in contemporary human rights discourse that would validate their demands is surprising. This is because, despite Roosevelt's promises, not only the existence of such an element but also its very legitimacy were for many years very effectively obscured and denied as western philosophers sought to demonstrate with remarkable uniformity either that only the array of rights contained in the UDHR or even that only civil and political rights were truly important and/or universal. Sometimes this was done with a strong sense of what was at stake in the cold war, as in the cases of Isaiah Berlin's (1958) argument for the UDHR's array and Maurice Cranston's (1967) argument for the privileging of civil and political rights. More often, however, there is little direct or even circumstantial evidence of any such committed engagement.

Berlin's argument on behalf of the UDHR began by distinguishing between negative liberties, or such freedoms from state interference as are instanced by civil and political rights, and positive liberties, or such freedoms to do things as are supported by states who are committed to the realisation of economic and social rights. It concluded in the manner of the American Social Modernists, by arguing that, whilst negative liberties are more fundamental than positive liberties, there is nevertheless a need for the constraints on individual freedom implicit in state action on behalf of the positive liberties specified in the UDHR. This is in order both to prevent a repeat of the excesses of the laissez-faire period and to assure equality of opportunity. Cranston's argument for the privileging of civil and political rights was more directly dismissive of claims made on behalf of any other types of rights in that he argues that economic and social rights, for example, simply fail to meet the criteria that would allow one to designate them as human rights, which he specifies as 'universality', 'paramountcy', and 'practicality'. Thus, in his view, economic and social rights are neither necessary for everyone, especially important, nor practically feasible in many countries (for a careful critique, see Jones, 1994, p. 157 ff.). More abstractly, there was also Robert Nozick's later and less direct, libertarian, but equally ideologically engaged, argument that respect for civil and political rights logically excludes the possibility of economic and social rights insofar as the latter require the state to levy taxes and so impose forced labour on taxpayers (Nozick, 1974, p. 169).

The authors of the less obviously engaged arguments for the universality of the UDHR tended to be adherents to the liberal, Protestant variant of the natural rights tradition, who, for similar reasons to Berlin, appear to have felt obliged to qualify or complicate their understandings of the 'state of nature' in order to allow the universality of at least some minimal economic and social rights. Thus Alan Gerwith (1978) added 'well-being' to 'freedom' as the most basic of rights since they are both equally necessary for the voluntariness of individual action that, like Kant, he sees as essential if there is to be any morality at all. In his early and now classic work, *A Theory of Justice*, John Rawls (1971) achieved a similar position but inverted the argument by starting with equality and adding freedom. Thus he argued that, although, contrary to Locke, individuals contemplating the 'original position' from behind a 'veil of ignorance', which deprived them of any knowledge of the actual inequalities between them, would agree to distribute 'primary goods' – liberties, powers, opportunities, income and wealth and self-respect – equally in order to be sure to give themselves the best chance in life, they would nevertheless also accept a justification for inequality which almost completely undermined any presumption of equality. The need for such a justification arose from the further supposed agreement on the part of those in the original position that some people will always make more of their 'talents' than others. The name Rawls gave to his justification for inequality was the 'difference principle': 'social and economic inequalities are to be arranged so that they are . . . to the greatest benefit of the least advantaged' (ibid., p. 83). In capitalist societies, however, the unceasing accumulation of wealth is the *sine qua non* of the whole system with the result that, willy nilly, some of the increased wealth is likely to 'trickle down' and so benefit the least advantaged in an absolute sense, which means that nothing need ever be done about inequality.

What all of these positions had in common and what in philosophical terms ultimately explains their shared though varying degrees of animosity towards the value of reciprocity is their privileging of individual autonomy as an empirical as well as a moral fact. This, then, is not only why civil and political rights ultimately always took precedence over economic and social rights for the first three generations of postwar western philosophers, but also why it is so hard for those who follow them today to see that neither civil and political rights nor even the UDHR as a whole pass muster as instances of the *ius cosmopoliticum* – surely, they ask rhetorically, there is nothing more obviously universal and therefore cosmopolitan than the autonomy of the human individual?

The answers to this question provided by the campaigns for the 'new universalism' may be summarised as variations on an Orwellian theme in that each of them, for different reasons, seems to be saying that, whatever its claims to the contrary, contemporary human rights discourse is not in fact cosmopolitan, since, because it very clearly privileges autonomy over reciprocity, it also allows some individuals to be more autonomous than others. More specifically, on the topic of personhood, the reason for the

UDHR's lack of concern with the particular oppressions that affected non-white peoples is easy enough to understand in that it reflected a combination of the racism intrinsic to western cultures (Banton, 1977; Bessis, 2003; Jordan, 1974) and a certain embarrassment at the ethical dissonance produced by support for the UDHR, on the one hand, and the maintenance of colonies or, in the United States, segregation, on the other – best, therefore, to avoid the matter. In the case of women, the failure of international human rights discourse to address their concerns is somewhat harder to understand since, of course, many white westerners are women. Until, that is, it is realised that gender discrimination was so taken for granted by the authors of the UDHR and the Covenants that no one realised there was a problem about confining the applicability of human rights to the public sphere of courts, politics, work and welfare, until this was pointed out by feminist scholars (Smart, 1989). Moreover, once the private sphere of relationships and families was opened up to interrogation in terms of human rights, it was discovered that women's problems where not reducible to instances of discrimination in the public sphere (Charlesworth, 2000) but included, not just *sui generis* private abuses such as domestic violence and those associated with reproductive issues (Butegwa, 1995), but also *sui generis* public sphere issues that follow from women's 'special' status in many cultures as mothers, wives and daughters (Cook, 1994; Schuler, 1995). For all these reasons, then, it was necessary for human rights to be gendered through the addition of the Convention on the Elimination of All Forms of Discrimination Against Women (CEDAW) to the canon. Finally, the continuing interrogation of the private sphere eventually led to the raising of the issue of the relationship between sexual orientation and human rights. Here the reason for the failure of the human rights canon to include sexual minorities in the list of groups protected against discrimination in respect of their human rights reflects not just the taboos operant at the time they were written but also a fear or prejudice that is still very deeply rooted in many parts of the world (Clapham, 1993; Donnelly, 2003, ch. 13).

As regards information and communications, the reason the core texts proved to be insufficient was simply because technological, economic and social developments rendered the provisions relating to freedom of expression anachronistic very soon after they came into force. In other words, no one in 1948 had any idea how quickly new and extraordinarily powerful means of circulating information around the globe would become established. It is to the great credit of Southern journalists, academics, and some politicians and international civil servants at the UN and UNESCO that they so rapidly and effectively realised the significance of these dramatic technological advances for informational inequality – simple cost would exclude the South from full or even any sort of active participation in the newly enhanced global information flows (see UNESCO's McBride Commission Report of 1980 and its proposals for a New World Information Order). Unfortunately, the United States and Britain temporarily left UNESCO in protest at the threat to private interests posed by the proposals. As predicted, and notwithstanding the recent emergence of al-Jazerra, the result of the consequently ever deepening informational inequality and exclusion is that the South cannot speak directly to the North and the North's representations of the South tend to be oversimplified – either over-exoticised or largely negative – and seldom include any acknowledgement of Northern responsibilities for any of the disasters commonly portrayed (Davis, 2002). Indeed the problem of informational inequality is now recognised to be even more profound in that it extends to access, or more often lack of it, to the most basic communicative technologies, whether for sending or receiving (Hamelink, 1994).

Concerning the different modes of social life, the demand is that international human rights discourse should acknowledge them much more fully, in order that individuals should be equally effectively protected throughout the world irrespective of the regime under which they live. This demand has been put with the greatest force by the proponents of 'Asian Values' . Reflecting the continuing influence of the western philosophical positions outlined above, the Asian Values argument has more often been seen as a threat to human rights than a way of making the protections they offer more widely available. However, when one looks at all but the most extreme variants of the 'Asian Values' argument with a little care, one discovers that whilst there is indeed a great deal of criticism of western hypocrisy in the application of human rights standards and a more general suspicion of the West's intentions in applying them, there is no overall intellectual rejection of human rights nor even of civil and political rights (Langlois, 2001). Thus, with respect to civil and political rights, there are no widely supported, principled rejections of the protections provided in relation to the physical integrity of individuals, the legal process, nor even of the idea that such rights should be equally available irrespective of religion or gender. Nor is there any intellectual rejection of the right to political participation. There are, though, amongst certain Islamic writers, for example, different understandings concerning the nature of 'cruel and unusual punishments', and resistances to allowing believers the freedom to give up their faith and women to choose their husbands. And more generally, there is a fear of the possibly negative consequences for social order and successful development of 'excessive' freedoms in the areas of expression and association. More positively, the proponents of Asian Values point to social order, hierarchy, benevolence, duty and loyalty as additional or alternative sources of virtue, and therefore of rights and wrongs. In my view (Woodiwiss, 1998; 2003), if not always that of the original proponents, such values ought to be incorporated into international human rights discourse if it is to regarded as more truly cosmopolitan.

Some of these virtues, notably those validating social order and hierarchy, already inform international human rights discourse. Thus it is well established that rights should not endanger social order and, as I have argued above (see p. 6), the very idea of rights assumes, and to that degree validates, the existence of hierarchies that may result in abuse. However, the other and more positive non-western values related to the principle of reciprocity have no place in international human rights discourse. As a result no protection is available when states or superiors more generally fail to do their duty, act benevolently, or reward loyalty. The ultimate source of these absences from international human rights discourse is the deeply entrenched liberal and indeed socialist as well as orientalist western view – significantly, although seldom mentioned these days, Locke's *Second Treatise* was an explicitly anti-familialist argument – that such behaviours were and are aspects of social relationships that were and are traditionalist and *therefore* inherently oppressive. However, the fact remains that the majority of the world's population, and not simply people living in Asia, still depends for protection upon the consistent enactment of such behaviours and therefore the underlying vivacity of the values that inform them (cp. Asad, 1996, p. 285). Thus to exclude these values from international human rights discourse is both to diminish the local effectiveness of what we like to call 'traditional' means of individual and social defence and to deny to the global majority what little protection global institutions can provide. What is more, the baleful effects of these absences are particularly likely to be felt when the capitalism spawned in part by the same individualism and liberalism arrives in the lands of the majority (cp. Rajagopal, 2003, p. 2).

Turning to the difference of status between justiciable civil and political and the supposedly merely programmatic economic and social rights, one is immediately struck by problems with the reasoning behind it. Economic and social rights were ostensibly assigned programmatic rather than justiciable status both because no court could be expected to be able to will the resources necessary to make them a reality and in order not to impose too great an economic burden on developing societies. However, no court can will the very substantial resources necessary to support a legal system either. Moreover, to say that even such a minimal and cheaply deliverable entitlement as a right to 'adequate housing', for example, is not justiciable cannot mean that it could not in principle be pursued through the courts since all such a possibility would require would be appropriately drafted legislation, for which many models exist in the statute books and administrative regulations of the more developed societies. Rather, what it does mean is that there is no international legal requirement for the existence of such legislation. One result, then, of the diminished status of economic and social rights is that any response to need is therefore left to the discretion of governments and their calculations of political advantage. Another result is that, since Article 1 of the ICESCR defines the resources available for development as including those made available 'through international assistance and co-operation, especially economic and technical', there is also no possibility that the richer countries could be legally held to account with respect to the level of assistance they provide.

Finally and developing the last point, when one considers the campaigns around the right to development and indigenous rights, one directly encounters the effects of the already discussed exclusions with respect to autonomy on the role allowed to reciprocity within current human rights discourse. The first of these effects is represented by the stalling of the formerly very substantial political and intellectual campaign for a right to development that would have required northern countries to commit significant resources to southern development activities. Because of persisting racism, lack of concern for the special difficulties of women in the South, who risk social ostracism or worse if they assert their autonomy, negative stereotyping of southern societies in much of the media, lack of respect for non-western ethical systems, and the absence of any obligation on either southern or northern governments to enhance respect for economic and social rights, it would have been very surprising if there had been any other result. The second and more explicit effect of these exclusions on the recognition of reciprocity is represented by the equally unsurprising stalling of the campaign for the recognition of the rights of indigenous peoples. Those who have argued against the recognition of indigenous rights have done so in a number of ways: by pointing to the extraordinary diversity amongst the peoples concerned and on this basis calling into question the very possibility of such a category of persons let alone rights; by arguing that there are no *sui generis* indigenous rights that could not be protected by deploying the existing array of human rights; by claiming that indigenous rights are collective rather than individual rights and so do not qualify as human rights; and finally, by equating advocacy of indigenous rights with the supposed great sin of the human rights world, namely cultural relativism (Thornberry, 2002, pp. 2–8). As Thornberry shows, all of these criticisms can be both effectively countered and the indigenous position in fact advanced through the existing human rights instruments and mechanisms. However, as he concludes:

> [H]uman rights are double-edged . . . There are losses and gains in trading in the currency of human rights . . . As indigenous peoples structure their claims in the language of human rights, so human rights structure the modes of social representation and the potential responses. *The individual rights 'grid' or syntax of human rights makes difficult the case for the collective* . . . Human rights set apparent limits to the kind of social practices embraced. Human rights is still infused with notions of progress and civilisation.
>
> (Thornberry, 2002, p. 428, emphasis added)

What Thornberry means by 'the collective' is what I have been referring to as reciprocity or the chthonic principle.

SOCIOLOGY AND THE REDISCOVERY OF RECIPROCITY

Clearly, there is a lot at stake in the battles over the 'new universalism'. To repeat Howard Becker's famous question to sociologists in the 1960s, 'Whose side are we on?' Even though this sounds more like a political than a sociological question, it is nevertheless an appropriate one since the current work of sociologists in the human rights area is in fact highly, if sometimes somewhat obliquely, engaged. In Chapters 2 and 4, I outlined what I regard as the principal historical contributions made by sociologists to the study of rights. At this point it is important to acknowledge that the writers involved would not have described their work as contributions to the field of human rights. For the nineteenth-century writers this was, of course and most obviously, because no such field of enquiry existed. Also, the silence of post-1945 sociologists reflected a continuation of their predecessors' deep scepticism as regards the meaningfulness and ideological significance of the concept of natural rights and a preference for the apparently more concrete language of citizenship and the welfare state. Thus there is something of a mystery as to why there should have been a sudden efflorescence of work describing itself as contributing to a sociology of human rights in the mid-1990s. This is not the place to engage in any sort of sociology of sociology, so it will have to suffice to say that this efflorescence appears to have been the result of a combination of factors that, in Foucaultian terms, changed the nature of the discursive formation. These included the end of communism, the intellectual foregrounding of globalisation, the emergence of sociological approaches that take discursive phenomena more seriously than had been the case in the past, and the suddenly more communitarian nature of human rights talk itself. Of these factors, the end of communism and the appearance of the new communitarianism were perhaps the most pertinent to explaining the engaged character of the work that is about to be described. This is because all of this work seems, to me at least, to be animated by a desire to counter what might be described as the socially 'thin' ethics associated with a triumphalist neo-liberalism; that is, what one sees in the contemporary sociology of human rights is a repetition of the Marxist critique of 'bourgeois right', but from within rights discourse as a revival of the minor tradition rather than from without.

The person who first broke the sociological taboo against taking human rights seriously was Bryan Turner (1993), and he did so in a rather dramatic fashion; that is, by producing a sociological argument for 'natural or inalienable rights'. As Turner explains, and as was illustrated in Chapter 2 above, not only Marx but Durkheim and Weber too insisted that the primary task of sociology was to account for the presence and provenance of certain values in particular societies at particular times rather than to generate or elaborate upon them. Hence, as illustrated in Chapter 4 of this text, the strong preference amongst subsequent generations of sociologists for the concept of citizenship over that of rights. However, as Turner also points out, the work of the classical sociologists was shot through with positive value commitments which became especially explicit whenever they wrote about how contemporary social conditions might be ameliorated. The sources of these values, if not the values themselves, he continues, have gained a new salience as both the Eurocentrism of the concept of citizenship has become apparent (ibid., p. 497) and the idea of the powerful state with which citizenship is intimately connected has been challenged by the 'pressures of globalisation'. This salience arises because, counter-intuitively, the ethical tradition from which the classical sociologists drew their inspiration turns out to be of critical importance in the construction of a new form of solidarity beyond that associated with citizenship, namely 'human rights solidarity'.

For Turner, when compared with citizenship, this new form of solidarity is 'more universal' thanks to the international bill of rights which most nation states have signed up to, 'more contemporary' because human rights enforcement is not solely dependent on the actions of declining nation states, and 'more progressive' because the values involved 'are not related to the management of people by a state' (ibid., p. 498). Given the argument set out in the present text, each of these statements seems highly questionable until one realises that Turner does indeed derive his conception of human rights from the value stream from which the classical sociologists drew rather than from the values they criticised, namely individualism, private property and liberalism. More specifically, he derives his conception of human rights not from Locke *et al.* but from two very different sets of ideas. First, via Arnold Gehlen (1988), from Nietzsche's conception of human beings as 'not fully complete animals' and therefore as inherently 'frail' because of the prolonged period of childhood vulnerability consequent on their underdeveloped instinctual apparatus, and, it might be added, because of the ease with which they can be confined. Second, the complimentary idea of 'social precariousness' to be found in the writings of the classical sociologists whenever they stressed, which was often, the incapacity of social institutions to protect these frail creatures fully.

In other words, as a conscious attempt to produce a globally applicable ethic that is both mindful of what individuals have in common – frailty – and respectful of social difference – the institutions that fail to protect people are very varied – Turner's conception of human rights represents a supersession of the liberal and indeed social-democratic traditions. The latter traditions share what Locke and Kant regarded as an inevitably ethnocentric republicanism in that they specify the solution at the same time as they identify the problem: the lack of liberty requires its institutionalisation, and economic and social needs require mechanisms for meeting them. By contrast, Turner's conception implies a cosmopolitan aspiration in that, like Barrington Moore (see above, p. 46), he stresses humanity's common misery and does not specify how it should be best alleviated; that is, he simply suggests that the chthonic principle or reciprocity – 'collective compassion' – is the core value in that we all share a responsibility to alleviate each other's misery, and he therefore allows the thought that there is no one best way in which this should be done.

Although it contains no direct references to Turner's work, Fred Twine's *Citizenship and Social Rights* (1994) develops several of the same themes, notably that concerning the search for a contemporary rationale for the principle of reciprocity or what he terms 'social interdependence'. However, whereas Turner finds this rationale in the shared danger of misery, Twine suggests what form this misery might take in that he finds the rationale for reciprocity in the shared threat to our sense of 'self' that arises when we are forced to be self-reliant, are careless of the consequences of our actions for others, neglect the importance of the unpaid labour of others, especially women, in caring for children and old people, or tolerate the social exclusion of others because they are poor. For Twine, then, there is no antagonism between self-development and reciprocity where the latter is understood to involve interacting with, respecting, valuing and sharing with others. This is because, contrary to the views of the 'autonomy' theorists, these activities rather precisely represent the opportunities and disciplines necessary for the self-development of socially interdependent creatures: 'human lives are essentially moral or they are nothing' (ibid., p. 3).

What turns this into the beginnings of a cosmopolitan argument rather than simply a republican defence of the welfare state is Twine's recognition that the finite nature of the world's resources and the fragility of its ecosystem mean that more people need the social rights provided by the welfare state than the planet can afford. The result is that in his view the fulfilment of the reciprocal obligations of the developed towards the less developed countries extend far beyond the provision of aid to encompass a 'change in [developed countries] value orientations . . . away from 'having' towards 'being' (ibid., p. 4) and increased, as well as increasingly multilateral, democratic participation in global social management. Thus, for Twine, the social interdependence that is necessary to individual as well as social development implies the 'social development of all' or generalised equality, which aspiration he considers worthy of being 'a secular "object of devotion"' (ibid., p. 6) or, in other words, sacred.

An even more explicitly cosmopolitan argument in the minor tradition is to be found in the Portuguese sociologist Boaventura de Sousa Santos' vivid and panoramic *tour de force, Towards a New Common Sense* (1995). In his Conclusion Santos both poses and tries to answer the question 'Can law be emancipatory?' In Santos' view, it is necessary to pose the question because in the West, where it originated, rights discourse, whether in the form of 'neo-liberalism' or 'demosocialism', appears to have exhausted its emancipatory potential and become a central component of a 'contractualist', neo-liberal mode of governance that excludes more people than it includes and which he therefore describes as 'social fascism'. In arriving at what nevertheless turns out to be a positive answer to his question about law's emancipatory potential, Santos depends upon what he terms a 'sociology of emergences.' On this basis he claims to descry the beginnings of a 'counter-hegemonic' movement articulating a 'sub-altern cosmopolitanism' that will eventually restore the law's capacity to contribute to a presently still inchoate emancipatory project that he understands as a global 'conviviality' ruled by the twin principles of equality and respect for difference. As Santos happily acknowledges, the incoherence of this imagined project is readily apparent in the very obvious diversity of the groups and/or social developments that he associates with it: Mexico's indigenous Zapatistas, non-citizens such as refugees and illegal migrants, and the postcolonial revival of indigenous and other modes of 'traditional' law. However, as theorised by the Zapatistas, the project's very inchoateness and incoherence explains its power since the 'social fascists' can never be sure where the next challenge will come from: will it be grounded, for example, in an authoritarian, hierarchist and highly legalistic traditionalist morality, as in the case of some varieties of contemporary Islam, Hinduism or Confucianism? Or will it take an anarchical, implicitly egalitarian and illegal form, as in the cases of the land invasions and electricity theft that frequently occur across the South and which for Santos foreshadow a new morality and therefore a new legality?

All of this problematises the present array and hierarchy of human rights in that Santos regards the currently restricted range of rights and the privileging of civil and political rights within this range as responsible for the denial of legitimacy to many efforts on behalf of the new conviviality. His solution is to argue for the recognition that there are many different 'languages' of human dignity and for the importance of translating them into each other's terms so as to make possible a 'virtuous hybridization' that will 'link local embeddedness and grassroots relevance . . . [with] translocal intelligibility and emancipation' and so legitimate the egalitarian actions associated with the cosmopolitan cause. The latter he considers best exemplified by: first, the 'rediscovery of labour' as a critically important democratic force in the making of a new 'global legality', thanks to the movements for reduced working hours, international labour standards, and against sweatshops; second, the legal protection of non-capitalist production; and, third, the 'participatory budgeting' exemplified by developments in the Brazilian city of Porto Alegre.

Another explicitly cosmopolitan text in the minor tradition is Johan Galtung's (1994) *Human Rights in Another Key*. Galtung makes essentially the same argument as Santos, but in a more abstract way. Thus Galtung points out that because of its western history, the spread of rights discourse both involves and depends upon the spread of far more than an ethic. This 'far more' includes: assumptions concerning the West's centrality to the spatial ordering of the planet; the westernised character of the world's imagined future; an ontological atomism according to which individuals and nation states are the basic units of local and global social relations respectively; a human-centred conception of nature; an ego-centred conception of the person; and, surprisingly, a supra-individual or 'transpersonal' conception of the 'norm-giver' (god, the state or the UN) (ibid., pp. 13–18). The spread of rights discourse is therefore both potentially profoundly imperialistic and in fact rather unlikely. It is unlikely not simply because these assumptions are not widely shared outside the West, but also because what is believed elsewhere is most often an opposite set of assumptions. In sum, for Galtung, like civil and political rights themselves, the assumptions that justify their privileging in the West are 'actor-oriented', whereas the assumptions that govern non-western conceptions of social justice are 'structure-oriented' and tend therefore to point to the meeting of collective needs and the privileging of economic and social rights. However:

> What we are looking for is the consistent translation of human rights thinking into local normative culture . . . Particular human rights, made specific to local culture and historical context, may be as significant as universal human rights. But one approach does not exclude the other. Both – and, not either – or.

(ibid., p. 113)

This said, at the global level Galtung is very clear both about the priority that should be accorded development and the obligations this imposes on the North vis-à-vis the South which are that, although responding to individual needs is a necessity, the establishment of locally controlled preventative structures (ibid., p. 114 ff) is the key to a prosperous and peaceful future unmarred by human rights abuses: 'Actor-oriented thinking leads to institutions to handle evil actors, structure/culture-oriented thinking to politics to change wrong structures and aggressive cultures' (ibid., p. 142). His conclusion, therefore, is that, although the evil individual should of course be prosecuted, in the long run it is more important to 'arraign the structure in court' (ibid., p. 143) and show, as in the great American desegregation case of *Brown* v. *Board of Education* (1954), how the structure 'works automatically to deprive large numbers of people of their human rights day in and day out, and how an alternative structure would produce better results from human rights points of view' (ibid., p. 144). This, of course is but a sociological repetition of what is involved in the campaigns for the new universalism.

From what has been said so far in this section, it should be clear that sociologists, or at least those few sociologists who write about human rights, have become very committed to the minor tradition with its stress on the principle of reciprocity as both an ideal and a real, operant social process. Given that sociology prides itself on being a reflexive discipline, it seems fitting that I end this section by outlining another argument produced if not fully completed in the mid-1990s. This is Stanley Cohen's investigation of why so few people amongst what others have termed the world's 'contented third' can bring themselves to act on the basis of such a commitment once they have attained it. As Cohen (2000) acknowledges, and in line with what one would expect given the human rights paradox, the reasons *why* we resort to denial have to do with our having some sort of interest in the continuation of the abuse, typically mediated through governments or economic agents of one kind or another, such as banks, manufacturers and supermarkets. However, since unfortunately little is ever done to correct the abuse, he focuses on *how* it is that we and our governments can know so much about 'atrocities and suffering' and do or even think so little about them. Thus he outlines and illustrates the many forms, levels and modes of denial that we deploy on our own behalves or collude in, before analysing the problems caused by the structures of denial for human rights activists. He ends by exploring how denial is or might be overcome and stresses that, although worrying about denial instead of engaging in political action may itself be a form of denial, a commitment to social justice does not require one to be a hero but instead simply 'discourages ordinary silence' (Cohen, 2000, p. 277).

CONCLUSION

The 1990s, then, saw the production of a body of sociological work on human rights that exhibited some striking differences when compared to that produced within such disciplines as philosophy and political theory. First and because, appropriately if perhaps a little too enthusiastically for an empirically orientated discipline, its practitioners have based their approach on popular understandings or expectations of human rights rather than textual exegesis, sociologists have become very open to a cosmopolitan reading of the minor tradition in human rights discourse. Second, and consequently, sociologists have also been both appreciative of the critiques of established human rights discourse associated with the campaigns for the new universalism and open to suggestions for the radical rethinking of the discourse. In sum, and despite the fact that the sociological presence in the human rights field is currently restricted to a small number of exploratory texts, the outline of a distinctive and potentially transformative approach to thinking about human rights is already apparent and has begun to be applied in an increasing number of more empirically focused studies such as Kevin Bales (1999) work on the 'new slavery' and my own on labour rights (Woodiwiss, 1998, 2003).

At the centre of this approach is an insistence that human rights have to be globally meaningful, effective and incorporate a strong sense of reciprocity, if they are not to be simply instances of overweening republican virtue, if they are not to be stimulants of denial. Hence, Turner's identification of our shared humanity with our bodily frailty and Twine's with our capacity for self-development, both of which are far less culturally specific than Kant's autonomy. Hence, the cosmopolitan nature of the moral imaginary that sacrilises this shared identity, however conceptualised, and as exemplified by Turner's '*collective* compassion', Twine's 'social interdependence', and Santos' 'global conviviality'. All of these conceptions of our moral universe are far more inclusive and communitarian than any conception of 'social contract' in that they all suggest that our moral responsibility for one another is both comprehensive and inescapable and therefore that there is no possibility of any nation state or region contracting out. Hence, finally, the recognition, especially apparent in Galtung's work, that, while the existing human rights regime – like the practice of human sacrifice in earlier times – may have played a very important role in initiating or making possible the idea of a global moral community, it too, alongside or even in tandem with uncontrolled capitalism or a resurgent western imperialism, may have become an obstacle to the further development of such a moral community and so be one of those structures that should be arraigned on charges that would include aiding and abetting those in denial by, for example, insisting that only civil and political rights are justiciable – there is no need to worry about poverty provided the poor are free.

CONCLUSION
For a new universalism

The politics of human rights deploys the symbolic or cultural capital of human rights to the ends of the management and distribution of power in national and global arenas . . .

No phrase except a romantic one – *the revolution in human sensibility* – makes the passage from a politics *of* human rights to a politics *for* human rights. That new form of sensibility, arising from responsiveness to the tortured and tormented voices of the violated, speak to us of an alternate politics seeking against heavy odds . . . that order of progress which makes the *state more ethical, governance progressively just, and power increasingly accountable.* The struggles which these voices name draw heavily on cultural and civilisational resources richer than those provided by the time and space of the Euro-enclosed imagination of human rights which they also seek to innovate.

(Baxi, 2002, p. 41, emphasis in original)

This book set out to answer a pair of interlinked questions: how did human rights become entangled with power relations? How might the nature of this entanglement be altered so that human rights better serve the global majority? The process of answering these questions began by locating the issues involved within the problematic of human sacrifice rather than that of the social contract. The figure of the social contract obscures the fact of the entanglement of rights discourse with power relations since it leads one to see rights both as the spontaneous product of an unforced consensus and as equally beneficial for all rights bearers. By contrast, in my view, the figure of human sacrifice fruitfully elucidates this entanglement by leading one to see rights not simply as an assertion of power that has unequal effects on different classes of bearers, but also as one that both requires sacrificial offerings to be made by those who would be rights bearers and provides subordinate individuals and groups with the means to assert themselves. More concretely, one is led to the following general conclusions:

First, given that historically rights arrived with capitalism, its specific social divisions, and its privileging of capital over the individual, freedom comes at a price in that it requires the sacrifice of control over one's labour power and a further dramatic weakening of the universal obligation to engage in mutual aid that governed social relations in chthonic societies;

Second, the conflicting groups of rights bearers and would-be rights bearers are forever trying to find unilaterally advantageous ways of overcoming the tension between the promises of protection and support that rights represent and the sacrifices required in return;

Third, this tension is irresolvable since the lost mutuality can never be fully restored despite the fact that some of the sacrifices demanded allow the continued violation of the same human sacredness that rights discourse claims to protect;

Fourth, despite the promises of protection and support they offer, but because of the social divisions that make rights both possible and necessary, the net effect of the arrival and enforcement of rights discourse is more likely to be endless strife than perpetual peace.

Within this transformed analytical context, the first question was answered by providing an historico-sociological account of the emergence and development of plain legal rights and their transmutation into human rights. Put in the broadest possible terms, the conventional histories of human rights begin with what, since Locke, has been imagined as the original state of freedom that preceded the drawing up of the social contract. Thereafter, the story is presented as an account of a steadily broadening resistance to the state's subsequent abuse of the social contract exemplified by a series of classic texts and culminating in the UN General Assembly's adoption of the UDHR in 1948. Reading such histories in the light of the alternative starting point represented by the figure of human sacrifice, one discovers that the story of rights in the sense of the legal disciplinary mechanism of interest to sociologists begins not with any social contract nor even with Magna Carta but with the social dislocation caused and represented by the emergence of a new form of economic organisation, capitalism. More specifically, the rights story begins with the requirement on the part of the new economic system to find a way to protect the prerogatives of ownership throughout the ever-lengthening circuits of capital – from the site of production, to the market, to the bank, and back again. Sensitised by this discovery, it becomes clear that what the conventional story presents as a cumulative and inherently ameliorative process in which one development more or less automatically led to another is the product of ideological hindsight since there was in fact no necessary connection between either the texts involved or the events they memorialise.

Thus:

1 Magna Carta played no civil libertarian role in English law until Sir Edward Coke opportunistically invoked it in the course of the famous defence of the new private property in his *Institutes of the Laws of England* (1628–44).

2 The 1688 *Bill of Rights* did little or nothing for the civil and political rights of the vast majority of the English people because it did not in anyway challenge the existing highly restrictive, property-based limitations on political participation, and granted freedom of expression only to members of parliament and, even then, only in parliament.

3 The great French and American Declarations of rights also privileged property owners. In addition, and as with habeas corpus, very few of the propertyless subsequently actually enjoyed any of the rights listed. This was either because one needed considerable financial resources to claim them or because one could not use them to protect one's capacity to speak or organise against property or indeed against many other powerful interests – hence the legal difficulties faced by trade unions during the nineteenth century throughout western Europe and North America.

4 In the American case, the practical irrelevance of the Bill of Rights was particularly obvious since it only applied to the federal government and not the state governments which were much more important to the lives of most Americans until the 1930s. In fact, Americans only gained some of these protections vis-à-vis state governments in the 1960s, thanks to Chief Justice Warren.

In sum, the conventional rendering of the history of rights discourse is highly misleading not only chronologically but also, and therefore, as regards the nature of the social conditions that produced it. That is, rights discourse was initially the product of conditions at a particular time and place, namely seventeenth-century Europe, rather than in any sense immanent in humanity.

One's response to the discovery that rights discourse has from the beginning been entangled with the defence of private property depends upon how one understands the relationship between power and freedom more generally. If one understands the relationship to be negative in that power necessarily limits freedom, as most liberals and indeed sociologists have done since Locke, then rights, whether plain or human must be either inalienable or a sham depending on which of the positions – liberal or sociological – one takes. On the other hand, if one understands the relationship as positive in that freedom is the product of power, as Foucault argues in his work on governmentality, then it makes sense both to be sceptical about the claims made for rights and to pursue them. For Locke, freedom was an aspect of the natural condition of humanity before the existence of states, an aspect that had to be rediscovered, institutionalised and protected. By contrast, for Foucault, freedom was a very late development in human history that was the more or less accidental creation of states as they gained knowledge of their populations and tried to work out how to govern them.

Understood within Foucault's positive perspective, rights developed gradually in England and elsewhere in Europe as a means of protecting the disruptive interests of those who aspired to own property outside of the feudal tenurial chain and economically benefit from such ownership. In the seventeenth century an effort was made to dignify the core rights related to property and contract by retrojecting their existence back to the beginnings of human society, prior to the appearance of significant inequalities, and therefore prior also to the occurrence of rituals involving human sacrifice. This move was successful, not least because, apart from its intended effect, it also had the unintended effects of obscuring both the centrality of reciprocity to social development and the role of capitalism in the transformation of the basis of inequality in seventeenth- and eighteenth-century Europe. Moreover, since the rights involved were untarnished by any association with human sacrifice, they could be presented as absolute or inalienable. In this way, then, rights discourse gained its paradoxical character in that it comprised a combination of a promise of liberty for all with an insistence on the privileging of the holders of capital. The result was that, whatever other protections they provided, the core freedoms for a long time could not be used to challenge a major source of rights abuse, namely capitalist private property.

However, the social contract theorists who carried out the retrojection developed their ideas in opposition not only to those of feudal privilege but also in opposition to the 'communism' of seventeenth-century English groups such as the Ranters and Diggers. For the 'major tradition' within rights discourse that the social contract theorists initiated, the rights related to property and contract represented, in the literal sense of pictured, the means (that is, owning things and making agreements) by which the essential elements of humanity's supposed primordial liberty were preserved despite the recognition of the need for social order. By contrast, for the 'minor tradition' that articulated the thought of Locke with that of the Diggers and Ranters, and was initially exemplified by the thought of the Levellers, humanity's original position was governed by the principle of reciprocity rather than that of liberty. The result was that the establishment of the same rights of property and contract as were celebrated by the major tradition was seen by the minor tradition as a severe challenge to freedom in the form of the danger that reciprocity might be replaced by selfishness as the core social value. Nevertheless, so strong were the economic and political desires animating both traditions and so powerful did the resulting myth – whether known as the 'ancient constitution' or 'the rights of man'- become, especially once it had been exported to continental Europe and the colonies and consequently articulated with other sources of antagonism towards the *ancien regime*, that the myth soon gained sacred status for itself as believers sacrificed themselves in the course of the various uprisings and revolutions that occurred in the seventeenth and eighteenth centuries.

Although rights discourse continued to inspire those still struggling against absolutism and feudalism across western Europe and elsewhere during the nineteenth century, it lost much of its inspirational quality in the societies where it was most thoroughly embedded, notably Britain, France and the United States. This was because in these societies, and apart from gradual, technical improvements in the administration of justice and trial procedures in criminal cases (Langbein, 2003), the propertyless were unable to gain access to most of the protections represented by civil rights and had to be largely content with their freedom to choose where to work and for whom to work. Nor did they get very far when they demanded political rights, whether as Chartists in England or the voteless supporters of Workingmen's parties in the north-eastern United States. The propertyless only gained political rights when the parties of the propertied decided they needed extra support in their struggles with each other. As a result and as the Diggers and Ranters had feared, in legal fact if not wider rhetorical terms, rights discourse became narrowly focused on the defence and extension of property rights as the core of what became aptly known as the *rule* of law. It was in this form that rights discourse was exported to the colonies and such subordinate states as Japan (that is, to most of the rest of the world).

All that said, the technical sophistication necessary to systematise rights discourse and so produce and maintain the rule of law as a mode of governance eventually created the intellectual means – see especially the contribution of Hohfeld (above p. 82) – whereby it became possible to think that the law might one day become more than an instrument for the defence of property rights, that it might one day provide the means through which the principle of reciprocity could be restored if not to the centre of social life then at least alongside that of individual autonomy. And this is indeed what eventually happened thanks to the changes in the social and political context of the law summarised by, in some cases, the emergence of trade unions and socialist parties articulating the minor tradition, as in western Europe, or, in others, the fear of their emergence, as in the United States. In this way, then, rights discourse had regained at least some its seventeenth- and eighteenth-century popular allure by the time the United States decided to join the war against fascism in 1941 and was therefore available to provide the strikingly inclusive language President Roosevelt used to outline the war aims of the United States.

Although it is in many ways a continuation of the broader story of rights, the more specific story of human rights is in another way the reverse of that of plain rights. That is, if the plain rights story is of a useful but narrow and profane idea that became more inclusive and even belatedly gained a certain patina of sacredness, the human rights story is of an initially sacred and broadly inclusive text, the UDHR, gaining some profane utility but having its meaning narrowed in the process. Despite all the politicking that attended its birth, international human rights began as a text made sacred by its status, in part at least, as the memorial for the millions of victims of what the preamble to the UDHR terms 'barbarous acts'. As such, and since in the preamble Roosevelt's 'Four Freedoms' – 'freedom of speech and belief and freedom from fear and want' – were also promised to the 'common people', it was also a promise of atonement on the part of its state signatories. The Nazi Holocaust was the act that the authors most obviously had in mind, but the generality of the language used implicitly extended the Universal Declaration's condemnation to all states since it seems to recognise that all are, *ipso facto*, capable of barbarous acts. Moreover, although the burden of atonement initially fell on the defeated Axis Powers, especially Germany and Japan, which were obliged to enact its provisions immediately, the fact that the protections summarised by the four freedoms were promised to the 'common people' of the world, suggests both a recognition of the principle of reciprocity and that the burden thereby assumed was to be shared by all other states and perhaps especially those most responsible for the fact and content of the UDHR, namely the major western powers.

One way, then, of summarising the story told in Chapter 9 is that it is an account of the West's, and especially the United States', attempt to free itself of the obligations, especially the economic obligations, it had assumed when it participated in the composition and approval of the UDHR. As was indicated in Chapter 7, this effort began with the very publication of the UDHR, since the key economic promise made in Roosevelt's 'Four Freedoms' speech, and the one most obviously inspired by the minor tradition, was not repeated in the UDHR. This was the promise of : 'freedom from want, which, translated into world terms, means economic understandings which will secure to every nation a healthy peacetime life for its inhabitants – everywhere in the world'. In its place are vague references to 'international co-operation' (Article 22) and a supportive 'international order' (Article 28). This retreat continued in the form of the rise of the doctrine of 'justiciability' (see above, p. 104), the associated privileging of civil and political over economic, social and cultural rights, and the consequent obscuring of the fact that something was already leeching away from the purportedly universal roster of rights, namely any at all strong sense of the reciprocity that has to be present if one wishes to describe any text as an instance of a *ius cosmopoliticum*.

Nevertheless, like the New Deal in relation to domestic American rights discourse, and to a significant degree for exactly the same American reasons, the passage of the UDHR represented the high-water mark of the minor tradition's influence on international human rights discourse. Thereafter, because of cold-war tensions and an anyway increasing American hostility to economic and social rights driven by the shift in the country's centre of political gravity to the right, the West in general and the United States in particular strove in one way or another to pre-empt any revival of the minor tradition's influence within human rights discourse. Thus the United States refused and still refuses to ratify the ICESRC or to support any campaigns for so-called 'third generation' rights, whilst at the same time energetically promoting a pre-emptive, property-centred 'New Constitutionalism' within the global economic institutions that it dominates. This said, as I have also tried to stress by discussing American domestic developments in some detail, civil rights, even more than polit-ical rights, simply are human rights for most Americans. Thus, if human rights in general are a means or technique of governance, as I have argued, then human rights for Americans are understood as a very specific set of such means or techniques. This very specific set of techniques is what most

Americans are culturally primed to think about when they hear the term human rights and it virtually exhausts what they know about and in which they have expertise. In other words, Americans are just as much captives of their own culture as any other peoples, and are therefore similarly challenged by the world's ongoing globalisation.

GLOBALISATION: THREAT OR OPPORTUNITY?

Globally these are interesting, dangerous and therefore challenging times. This is not simply because there is a very obvious lack of clarity as to what exactly globalisation might mean for the planet, but also because this lack of clarity appears to be unacceptable to an increasing number of political actors. More particularly but to simplify, an interesting and long-running debate about whether globalisation refers to a gradual process of multilaterally governed global integration or a new kind of empire has suddenly become rather threatening because, since the beginning of the overt preparations for the attack on Iraq, the political associations of the two theories have been reversed. Thus an anti-globalisation movement that was formerly guided by the imperialism thesis has become a staunch defender of multilateral global governance, whilst some pro-globalisation states, notably the United States and Britain, appear to have given up their erstwhile multilateralism and acknowledged what they regard as the necessity of imperialism (Cooper, 2002; Ignatieff, 2001). What makes these shifts a source of danger are: first, a thesis, that globalisation equals imperialism, which was formerly deployed for critical and defensive purposes has been transformed into a rationale for affirmative and offensive actions; second, the thesis now has great military power behind it; and, third, the thesis remains, in my view, a mistaken one. The net result of the change in the political associations of the imperialism thesis is therefore much more likely to be endless war than a rapidly achieved hegemonic tranquillity since, notwithstanding the availability of great force, globalisation has rendered imperialism impossible, as the presently unfolding Iraqi debacle so graphically illustrates.

However, rejection of the imperialism thesis does not mean that one should take up the integrationist alternative with its excessive stress on globalisation as involving the displacement of particularistic national and/or local social relations by universalistic, transnational social flows. This is because, in my view, globalisation is better understood as an emergent property of the international system produced by the *inability* of states, including so-called super powers, corporations and cultural producers to solve certain of their problems within the confines of existing national and international structures (Murphy, 1994; Woodiwiss, 2001, pp. 176–94). Globalisation, then, is an instance of what Marcel Mauss (1924) called a 'total social fact' in that it involves the fusion of many social elements and processes, in this case summarised as the local, the national, the international and the transnational. The result of this fusion is that there are occasions when developments along any one of these dimensions of the social may have consequences along the others that are normally beyond the capacity of national and international entities to control, no matter how powerful they may be. An obvious topical example of what would be commonly regarded as the least likely class of such events – a world-changing non-western development along the national dimension – was the Taliban's take-over of Afghanistan and the opportunity it provided for *al-Qaeda*.

When I say that the internal dynamics of a globalising world are 'normally beyond the capacity of national and international entities to control', I do not mean that they are inherently uncontrollable, but only that they cannot be controlled by the methods of geopolitical 'business as usual' as exemplified by such pre-globalisation strategies as are summarised by the term imperialism, whether of the go-it-alone or UN-mediated variety. More specifically, I mean that the internal dynamics of globalisation can only be controlled through being prepared to be engaged in unusual business, such as that Thomas Kuhn (1970) identifies as resulting from paradigm changes in the natural sciences and the consequent discovery of new entities, processes, relationships, and exemplary ways of working.

The relevance of all this to the sphere of human rights is that the paradigm that has guided our thoughts, actions and institution-building in the area since 1948 is in a state of crisis (cp. Brysk, 2002, conclusion; Falk, 2003, ch. 7). This is for four reasons. First, in the absence of any broader and more positive, internally generated ideology, American Administrations since President Carter's in the late 1970s have adopted an attenuated version of the UN's Civil and Political Covenant as their discourse of global 'leadership'. As Secretary of State, Colin Powell put it in his preface to his department's *Country Reports on Human Rights Practices* for 2002:

> The year began with American forces in combat in Afghanistan, and we continue to act there – with military, political and economic resources – to reverse the ill effects of the Taliban regime and the conditions that left unchecked its cruel disregard for human rights. Elsewhere in the world, *we set our sights on further extending the blessings of liberty and*

> *security*, and demonstrating not only that they are compatible, but also interdependent. We advanced these goals not as exclusively American aspirations, but rather as the birthright of all persons . . . In a world *marching* toward democracy and respect for human rights, the United States is a leader, a partner and a contributor. We have taken this responsibility with a deep and abiding belief that human rights are universal. They are not grounded exclusively in American or Western values. *But their protection world-wide serves a core U.S. national interest.*
>
> (Emphasis added)

Second, and as a consequence of being entangled with an imperialist project – 'we set our sights on further extending the blessings of liberty and security' – the *march* towards respect for human rights is leading to the multiplication of wrongs, witness the thousands of innocent civilian victims of the impetuous attacks on Serbia, Afghanistan and, most recently, Iraq that were launched in the name of the civil and political rights now commonly summarised as 'freedom'. Third, in conflict with American aspirations, recognition is being demanded for the fact that values other than those of individualism or indeed socialism may/should be the source of rights claims. These are the values of the non-west and most assertively of Asia; that is, the values associated with Islam, Confucianism, Buddhism, Hinduism and, indeed, both Catholic and Orthodox Christianity as well as Judaism which point to duty, benevolence and loyalty as additional or alternative sources of virtue, and therefore of rights and wrongs. Fourth, and momentously, as many have long suspected, there is now global evidence that increased freedom for capital has negative consequences even for civil and political rights (Milner, 2002).

Clearly, we cannot hope to overcome the problems caused by the increasingly apparent global unacceptability of the *privileging* of capitalist private property within human rights discourse by returning to chthonic modes of social organisation in any literal sense. Of course we should be much more respectful of those peoples who still live under at least a hybrid variant of such conditions. And one mark of such respect would be a broadening of the terms of reference and jurisdictions of the various UN human rights tribunals currently sitting in Africa so that they could examine the role of, for example, colonial administrations and armaments companies in the aetiology of the gross violations they are considering. In the absence of any such broadening, these tribunals, their judgments, and their sentences, like those of Nuremberg and Tokyo at the end of the Second World War (Sellars, 2002, chs 2 and 3), will be vulnerable to subsequent delegitimisation on the basis that they applied double standards.

However, we also owe it to our western selves as well as our co-inhabitants of the planet to find ways to resolve the paradox of human rights or at least to loosen further the connections between capitalist private property and rights discourse which have produced and maintained the paradox. In other words, difficult though it may be to see how this might be politically achieved, we owe it to ourselves to investigate and do something about the problem of inequality. Given this obligation, I would like to end by speculating on the possible future significance of the campaigns for what I have termed the 'new universalism' by pointing to some similarities between nineteenth-century and present-day conditions as they relate to rights.

In the nineteenth century and responding to their minor-tradition understandings of the word 'right', many of the propertyless of western Europe and North America appear, with the benefit of hindsight, to have in fact taken on board the arguments of political and legal philosophers to the effect that only the possession of property could qualify someone as a fitting recipient of civil and political freedoms. Thus, as the Legal Realists taught (see above, p. 83), in demanding economic and social rights, the propertyless were also demanding their share of property right, but in the name of reciprocity and therefore their autonomy too. Soon after these economic and social rights were obtained, access to a greatly enhanced bundle of hitherto denied civil rights followed thanks to the creation of legal aid schemes of one kind or another. This encroachment on property right is also why some libertarian jurists like Nozick (1974) regard the taxation that pays for the delivery of economic and social rights as theft and as therefore imposing 'forced labour' on taxpayers.

However, the lawyers and philosophers of the nineteenth and early twentieth centuries were wrong in the practical advice they offered to the propertyless – wait patiently and trust the good intentions of the propertied to deliver rights for all when the time is right. By contrast, the propertyless were correct in their contrary conclusion – and not just correct in a sentimental, moral way but in tough-minded political terms. In other words, whilst, from the point of view of the state and the propertied, the conventional story of civil rights leading to political and then social rights is reasonably accurate, it is not accurate from the point of view of the propertyless. In Britain, for example, and starting with few if any effective rights in the late eighteenth century, the propertyless of necessity constantly challenged the 'rule of (property) law' and its accompanying rights talk as they engaged more or less continuously in illegal acts of one kind or another in the course of developing the egalitarian political programme that eventually came to be known as socialism. Pursuit of this programme in no matter how inchoate a form generated the desire necessary to pursue political rights. Once won, the political rights were eventually successfully used to establish the various economic and social rights associated with trade unions and the welfare state, which, in turn, finally produced the cultural confidence and state financial support necessary to turn the otherwise mythical civil rights of the propertyless into real techniques of self- and social-defence. To have followed the strategy proposed by the lawyers and philosophers would have resulted in an indefinite postponement, even though the expert knowledges of lawyers and philosophers were vital in making the aspirations of the propertyless both technically achievable and, to a degree, legitimate.

The situation faced by today's subaltern groups is structurally similar to that faced by the propertyless in the nineteenth century in that they formally possess many rights of which they cannot make practical use. Responding this time to their own rather particular understandings of the meaning of the shift from talk of plain rights to talk of human rights ('human' is an inherently inclusive noun), subaltern groups of many types throughout the world have continued the minor tradition and read the use of this inclusive term as an encouragement to demand the same status and even the same standard of living as their supposed global betters. They too have often felt driven to engage in illegal actions in support of their causes. Thus inequality and the lack that it represents remains one of the principal sources of desire in social action. More specifically, the intrinsic referential ambiguity – does it refer to autonomy, reciprocity, or both? – of human rights discourse, plus the prizes it promises means that there is always something over and for which to fight. Indeed, the discourse's referential ambiguity has made it a veritable engine of challenges to the human rights status quo in that disagreements over the meaning of the central human rights texts have regularly led to subaltern groups finding something to fight for as they have attempted, in Galtung's sense, to arraign various structural relationships before the court of global public opinion. Thus, in the 1960s, non-white peoples, including many from newly independent countries, asked themselves if the discourse applied equally to them and, on finding that it did not do so explicitly enough, set about ensuring that it would do so in the future by successfully campaigning for the International Convention on the Elimination of All Forms of Racial Discrimination (ICEARD). Moreover, asking the same question initiated the campaigns for the 'new universalism', which if successful will enlarge the circle of reciprocity and so hugely increase the numbers of people whose autonomy will be recognised.

On this basis, then, and in line with what was suggested earlier concerning the critical and ameliorative possibilities that would be created by a more truly cosmopolitan human rights regime (see above, p. 0), it is possible to hope that we may also be approaching the discovery of a strategy for overcoming the current crisis in the human rights sphere. Such a strategy for loosening the connections between capitalist private property and rights discourse that produce and reproduce the paradox of human rights would have to include:

recognising that the present range of protected humans is only a selection from a far wider range of human types who should be protected;

recognising the necessity for rights to freedom of information and communication to the realisation of freedom of expression;

recognising the equal status to economic, social and cultural rights as compared to civil and political rights;

recognising claims to dutiful and benevolent treatment on the part of superiors as human rights;

recognising rights to development and for the protection of indigenous peoples.

Insofar as one of the eventual consequences of the successful achievement of such a programme would be a reduction of the share of the global economic surplus going to capital and an increase in that going to labour, it would represent as politically difficult and significant a challenge to the pre-eminence of capital internationally as that represented domestically by the arrival of the welfare state. Once again, then, encroaching on property right looks likely to be the key to loosening the social connections that maintain the human rights paradox and so to enhancing respect for human rights.

Of course, as Santos immediately recognised (see above, p. 132), any such strategy would also produce a mass of tensions, notably between the advocates of the rights of women or sexual minorities, on the one hand, and the advocates of patriarchalist or familialist values, on the other. What, however, may make the situation easier is the fact that it is well-established within human rights jurisprudence that one right cannot be used to justify the violation of another. This means that ways will have to be found to articulate these rights with one another. Fortunately, as was indicated in the main text, methodologies already exist for 'balancing' or 'harmonising' such discordant rights, and, most recently, for 'translating' (Woodiwiss, 2003) them into each other's terms. These methodologies are, or promise to be, highly effective, provided they are executed on the basis of an expertise grounded in what Turner (2002; see also, Nussbaum, 2002) has termed 'cosmopolitan virtue' – an ironic but respectful stance towards the values of one's own and other cultures. In sum, the answer to the question as to whether the nature of the entanglement of rights with power can be altered so that human rights better serve the global majority will have to wait for the results of the efforts to re-make human rights in a way that incorporates the ideas and demands associated with the campaign for the 'new universalism'.

All that said, it is also important to understand that there are certain inequalities that, as with those that allowed the occurence of human sacrifice, human rights cannot be expected to do away with; namely, those that made human rights possible in the first place, those that are intrinsic to the state and capitalism. Attending to these inequalities without putting individuals at even greater risk than they are presently therefore represents a challenge for societies and the social sciences more generally rather than for human rights, a great challenge.

NOTES

INTRODUCTION

1   The term 'reciprocity' is used here and throughout the text to refer to the set of obligations on individuals to engage in mutual aid that is generated by the inescapability of social interdependence. Today, the size and range of the set of mutual obligations formally recognised in any particular society largely depends upon the widely varying ways in which, and degrees to which, this interdependence is acknowledged by the state. Additionally, reciprocity provides the social grounding for most, if not all of the world's ethical systems in that it was and is the inspiration for the injunction commonly known as the 'golden rule': 'Do as you would be done by'.

2   Here I have in mind writings by Costas Douzinas (2000), Alain Badiou (2001), Perry Anderson (2002), Winin Pereira (1997), Chandra Muzaffar (1993), and the large group of eminent academic lawyers gathered together in Campbell *et al.* (2001).

3   Although I am highly critical of recent, so-called 'humanitarian interventions', this does not mean that I am opposed to such interventions in principle. However, as the law says of those seeking an emergency intervention through an injunction, those engaging in such interventions must 'come with clean hands' which rules out most national governments. This leaves the UN as the only body fit to take on such heavy responsibilities as the violation of sovereignty and the sacrificing of innocents (for an impressive attempt to further define and justify such a stance, see Lepard, 2002).

4   In order to avoid misunderstandings as to what is being claimed in

such a statement, it is perhaps important to make at least two points clear at the outset. First, although much of the book is concerned with developments in three particular societies, it does not provide a detailed account and assessment of the human rights records of these societies so much as use them as case studies to illustrate and explain in general terms how rights regimes or cultures have developed and differentiated. Second, although I consider the issues addressed and approach adopted here to be central to the sociology of human rights, they are, of course, by no means exhaustive of such a sociology.

1 THE PARADOX OF HUMAN RIGHTS

1   For a most enlightening discussion of the role of figures of speech in sociological work, see Lopez (2003).

6 JAPAN, THE RULE OF LAW AND THE ABSENCE OF LIBERTY

1   For Weber, patriarchalism was the elementary form of traditional authority and is defined as follows:

> [It] is the situation where, within a group (household) which is usually organised on both an economic and kinship basis, a particular individual governs who is designated by a definite rule of inheritance. The decisive characteristic . . . is the belief of the members that domination, even though it is an inherent traditional right of the master, must definitely be exercised as a joint right in the interests of all members and is thus not freely appropriated by the incumbent. In order that this shall be maintained, it is crucial that in both cases there is a complete absence of a personal (patrimonial) staff. Hence the master is still largely dependent upon the willingness of the members to comply with his orders since he has no machinery to enforce them. Therefore the members are not yet really subjects.
>
> (Weber, 1968, p. 231, emphasis added)

For Weber, then, patriarchalism was a strictly hierarchical political structure justified by a familialist discourse and resting on an economy and a wider set of social relations structured in large part by kinship.

7 THE UNITED STATES AND THE INVENTION OF HUMAN RIGHTS

1   This and the account of the later development of international human rights discourse in the UN included in Chapter 8 are taken from an already published account of UN developments that is organised on a much more explicitly Foucaultian basis (see Woodiwiss, 2002 and 2003, ch. 2).

9 THE UNITED NATIONS AND THE INTERNATIONALISATION OF AMERICAN RIGHTS DISCOURSE

1 What follows is derived from histories by Cassese (1990), Evans (1996), Lauren (1998), Luard (1982; 1989), Morsink (1999), Sellars (2002), Tolley (1987), and Vincent (1986), the comprehensive volume of texts and materials by Steiner and Alston (1996), and texts on enforcement by Alston (1992), Alston and Crawford (2000), and Flood (1998).

BIBLIOGRAPHY

Ackerman, B. (1991) *We the People: Foundations*, Harvard University Press, Cambridge, Mass.

Ackerman, B. (2000) *We the People: Transformations*, Harvard University Press, Cambridge, Mass.

G. Agamben, (1998) *Homo Sacer: Sovereign Power and Bare Life*, Stanford University Press, Stanford.

Akita, G. (1967) *Foundations of Constitutional Government in Modern Japan, 1868–1900*, Harvard University Press, Cambridge, Mass.

Ali, T. (2003) 'Re-Colonising Iraq', *New Left Review*, 21: 5.

Alston, P. (1992) 'The Committee on Economic, Social and Cultural Rights', in P. Alston, (ed.), *The United Nations and Human Rights: A Critical Appraisal*, Oxford University Press, Oxford.

Alston, P. and Crawford, J. (eds)(2000) *The Future of United Nations Human Rights Treaty Monitoring*, Cambridge University Press, Cambridge.

Amar, A. (2000) *The Bill of Rights*, Yale University Press, New Haven.

An-Naim, A.A. (1990) *Toward an Islamic Reformation: Civil Liberties, Human Rights and International Law*, Syracuse University Press, Syracuse.

Anderson, C. (2003) *Eyes off the Prize*, Cambridge University Press, Cambridge.

Anderson, P. (2002), 'Force and Consent – Aspects of US Hegemony', *New Left Review*, 17: 5.

Asad, T. (1996) 'On Torture, or Cruel, Inhuman, and Degrading Treatment', *Social Research*, 63: 14.

Atiyah, P.S. (1979) *The Rise and Fall of Freedom of Contract*, Oxford University Press, Oxford.

Auerbach, J. (1976) *Unequal Justice*, Oxford University Press, New York.

Austin, J. (1995) *The Province of Jurisprudence Defined*, Prometheus Books, New York.

Badiou, A. (2001) *Ethics: An Essay in the Understanding of Evil*, Verso, London.

Baker, J. (1979) *An Introduction to English Legal History*, Butterworth, London.

Bales, K. (1999) *Disposable People: New Slavery in the Global Economy*, University of California Press, Berkeley.

Banno, J. (1987) *The Formation and Collapse of the Meiji Constitutional System*, Orientation Seminar, 26, Japan Foundation, Tokyo.

Banton, M. (1977) *The Idea of Race*, Tavistock, London.

Bartholomew, A. and Breakspear, J. (2003) 'Human Rights as Swords of Empire', in L. Panitch and C. Leys (eds) *The New Imperial Challenge*, Merlin, London.

Bataille, G. (1973) *Theory of Religion*, Zone Books, New York.

Bauer, J. (2000) 'Human Rights for All? The Problem of the Human Rights Box', *Human Rights Dialogue*, 2(1): 1.

Bauer, J. and Bell, D. (eds) (1999) *The East Asian Challenge for Human Rights*, Cambridge University Press, Cambridge.

Baxi, U. (2002) *The Future of Human Rights*, Oxford University Press, New Delhi.

Beasley, W.G. (1972), *The Meiji Restoration*, Stanford University Press, Stanford.

Beckmann, G. (1957) *The Making of the Meiji Constitution*, University of Kansas, Lawrence.

Beer, L. (1968) 'The Public Welfare Standard and Freedom of Expression in Japan', in D. F. Henderson (ed.), *The Constitution of Japan: Its First Twenty Years*, University of Washington Press, Seattle.

Beer, L.W. (1984) *Freedom of Expression in Japan*, Kodansha International, Tokyo.

Beer, L. and Tomatsu, H. (1975) 'A Guide to the Study of Japanese Law', *The American Journal of Comparative Law*, 23: 284.

Bentham, J. (1782) *Of Laws in General*, reprinted in 1970 by Athlone Press, London.

Berger, R. (1969) *Congress Versus the Supreme Court*, Harvard University Press, Cambridge, Mass.

Berger, R. (1977) *Government by Judiciary*, Harvard University Press, Cambridge, Mass.

Berlin, I. (1958) *Four Essays on Liberty*, Oxford University Press, Oxford, reprinted 1969.

Berman, H. (1994) 'The Origins of Historical Jurisprudence: Coke, Seldon, Hale,' *Yale Law Journal*, 103(4): 1651.

Berman, H. and Reid, C. (1996) 'The Transformation of the English Legal

System: from Hale to Blackstone,' *Emory International Law Review*, 45(1): 437.

Bessis, S. (2003) *Western Supremacy: The Triumph of an Idea?*, Zed Books, London.

Bickel, A. (1970) *The Supreme Court and the Idea of Progress*, Harper and Row, New York.

Blackstone, W. (1765) *Commentaries on the Laws of England*, reprinted by University of Chicago Press, Chicago, 1979.

Brysk, A. (ed.)(2002) *Globalization and Human Rights*, University of California Press, Berkeley.

Burchell, G. and Gordon, C. (eds)(1991) *The Foucault Effect: Studies in Governmentality*, Harvester Wheatsheaf, London.

Butegwa, F. (1995) 'International Human Rights Law and Practice: Implications for Women', in M. Schuler (ed.) *From Basic Needs to Basic Rights: Women's Claim to Human Rights*, University of Pennsylvania Press, Philadelphia.

Cachan, M. (2002) 'Justice Stephen Field and Free Soil, Free Labor Constitutionalism: Reconsidering Revisionism', *Law and History Review* 20(3): 91, (Jul. 2004 <http://www.historycooperative.org/journals/lhr/20.3/forum_cachan.html>).

Caenegem, R.C. van, (1992) *An Historical Introduction to Common Law*, Cambridge University Press, Cambridge.

Cain, M. and Hunt, A. (eds) (1979) *Marx and Engels on Law*, Academic Press, London and New York.

Calabresi, G. (1982) *A Common Law for an Age of Statutes*, Harvard University Press, Cambridge, Mass.

Campbell, T., Ewing, K. and Tomkins, A. (2001) *Sceptical Essays on Human Rights*, Oxford University Press, Oxford.

Cardozo, B. (1920) *The Nature of the Judicial Process*, Yale University Press, New Haven.

Carter, J. (2003) *Understanding Sacrifice*, Continuum, London.

Cassese, A. (1990) *Human Rights in a Changing World*, Polity, Oxford.

Chandler, D. (2000) 'International Justice', *New Left Review*, 6: 55.

Chandler, D. (2002) *From Kosovo to Kabul: Human Rights and International Intervention*, Pluto, London.

Charlesworth, H. (2000) *The Boundaries of International Law: A Feminist Analysis*, Juris Publications Inc., New York.

Chase, W. (1982) *The American Law School and the Rise of Administrative Government*, University of Wisconsin Press, Madison.

Chen, P. (1981) *The Formation of the Early Meiji Legal Order*, Oxford University Press, Oxford.

Clapham, P. (1993) *Human Rights in the Private Sphere*, Oxford University Press, Oxford.

Coase, R. (1960) 'The Problem of Social Cost', *Journal of Law and Economics*, 3(1): 1.

Cohen, S. (2000) *States of Denial: Knowing about Atrocities and Suffering*, Blackwell, Oxford.

Collins, R. (1974) 'Three faces of cruelty,' *Theory and Society*, 1(2): 415.

Commons, J.R. (1924) *A History of Labour in the US*, Macmillan, New York.

Commons, J.R., Philips, U., Gilmore, E., Sumner, H. and Andrews, J. (eds) (1958) *A Documentary History of American Industrial Society*, vol. III, pt. 1, Russel and Russel, New York.

Cook, R. (ed.) (1994) *Human Rights of Women*, University of Pennsylvania Press, Philadelphia.

Cooper, R. (2002) 'Why we still need empires' in Foreign Policy Centre, *Reordering the World*, London.

Corbin, A. (1950) *Contracts*, reprinted in 1962 as *Corbin on Contracts: A Comprehensive Treatise on the Rules of Contract Law*, West, St. Paul, Minn.

Corwin, E. (1941) *Constitutional Revolution Ltd*, Pomona College, Claremont.

Cotterill, R. (1981) 'The Development of Capitalism, and the Formalisation of Contract', in B. Fryer, A. Hunt, D. McBarnet and B. Moorehouse (eds) *Law, State and Society*, Croom Helm, London.

Cover, R. (1975) *Justice Accused: Antislavery and the Legal Process*, Yale University Press, New Haven.

Cranston, M. (1967) *What Are Human Rights?*, Oxford University Press, Oxford.

Craven, M. (1995) *The International Covenant on Economic, Social and Cultural Rights*, Oxford University Press, Oxford.

Darian-Smith, E. and Fitzpatrick, P. (1999) *Modernism and the Grounds of Law*, Cambridge University Press, Cambridge.

Davis, M. (1986) *Prisoners of the American Dream*, Verso, London.

Davis, M. (2002) *Late Victorian Holocausts: El Niño Famines and the Making of the Third World*, Verso, London.

Davis, M.C. (ed.) (1995) *Human Rights and Chinese Values*, Oxford University Press, New York.

De Becker, J.E. (1909) *Annotated Civil Code of Japan*, reprinted by University Publications of America, 1979, Washington.

De Becker, J. (1916) *Elements of Japanese Law*, reprinted by University Publications of America, 1979, Washington.

Dicey, A.V. (1885) *Introduction to the Law of the Constitution*, reprinted by Palgrave Macmillan, London, 1985.

Donnelly, J. (2003) *Universal Human Rights in Theory and Practice*, second edition, Cornell University Press, Ithaca.

Douzinas, C. (2000) *The End of Human Rights*, Hart, Oxford.

Durkheim, E. (1957) *Professional Ethics and Civic Morals*, Routledge, London

Durkheim, E. (1964) *The Division of Labour*, Free Press, Glencoe.

Durkheim, E. (1976) *The Elementary Forms of the Religious Life*, Allen and Unwin, London.

Durkheim, E. (1982) *The Rules of Sociological Method*, Macmillan, Basingstoke.

Elias, N. (1978a) *The Civilizing Process I: The History of Manners*, Blackwell, Oxford.

Elias, N. (1978b) *The Civilizing Process II: State Formation and Civilization*, Blackwell, Oxford.

Ely, J.W. (1992) *The Guardian of Every Other Right: A Constitutional History of Property Rights*, Oxford University Press, New York.

Epps, C. (1998) *The Rights Revolution*, University of Chicago Press, Chicago.

Esping-Andersen, G. (1990) *The Three Worlds of Welfare Capitalism*, Polity Press, Cambridge.

Evans, T. (1996) *US Hegemony and the Project of Universal Human Rights*, Macmillan, Basingstoke.

Ewing, K. and Gearty, C. (2000) *The Struggle for Civil Liberties 1914–45*, Oxford University Press, Oxford.

Falk, R. (2000) *Human Rights Horizons*, Routledge, New York.

Falk, R. (2003) *The Great Terror War*, Arris Books, Moreton-in-the-Marsh.

Fine, S. (1964) *Laissez-Faire and the General Welfare State*, Ann Arbor Paperbacks, Ann Arbor.

Fitzpatrick, P. (2001) *Modernism and the Grounds of Law*, Cambridge University Press, Cambridge.

Flood, P.J. (1998) *The Effectiveness of UN Human Rights Institutions*, Praeger, Westport, Conn.

Foner, E. (1999) *The Story of American Freedom*, Norton, New York.

Foreign Policy Centre (2002) *Reordering the World*, London.

Foucault, M. (1972) *The Archaeology of Knowledge*, Tavistock, London.

Foucault, M. (1979) *The History of Sexuality, vol. 1*, Penguin, Harmondsworth.

Fox, A. (1974) *Beyond Contract: Work, Power and Trust Relations*, Faber and Faber, London.

Frank, J. (1930) *Law and the Modern Mind*, Coward-McCann, New York.

Frank, T. (2000) *One Market under God: Extreme Capitalism, Market Populism and the End of Economic Democracy*, Doubleday, New York.

Friedman, C. and Israel, F. (1969) *The Justices of the Supreme Court*, Bowker, New York.

Friedman, L.M. (1973) *A History of American Law*. Simon and Schuster, New York.

Friedman, W. (1964) *Law in a Changing Society*, Penguin, Harmondsworth.

Fryer, B., Hunt, A., McBarnet, D. and Moorehouse, B. (eds) (1981) *Law, State and Society*, Croom Helm, London.

Galtung, J. (1994) *Human Rights in Another Key*, Polity Press, Cambridge.

Garon, S. (1987) *The State and Labour in Modern Japan*, University of California Press, Berkeley.

Gehlen, A. (1988) *Man: His Nature and Place in the World*, Columbia University Press, New York.

Gewirth, A. (1978) *Reason and Morality*, University of Chicago Press, Chicago.

Gilmore, G. (1974) *The Death of Contract*, Ohio State University Press, Columbus.

Gilmore, G. (1977) *The Ages of American Law*, Yale University Press, New Haven.

Girard, R. (1979) *Violence and the Sacred*, Johns Hopkins University Press, Baltimore.

Girard, R. (1994) *Things Hidden Since the Beginning of the World*, Stanford University Press, Stanford.

Glendon, M.A. (1996) *Rights Talk: The Impoverishment of Political Discourse*, Free Press, New York.

Glendon, M.A. (2003) 'The Forgotten Crucible: The Latin American Influence on the Universal Human Rights Idea', *Harvard Human Rights Journal*, 16(2): 28–39.

Glenn, H.P. (2000) *Legal Traditions of the World*, Oxford University Press, Oxford.

Gluck, C. (1985) *Japan's Modern Myths: Ideology in the Late Meiji Period*, Princeton University Press, Princeton.

Goodman, R. and Neary, I. (eds) (1996) *Case Studies in Human Rights in Japan*, Curzon Books, Richmond.

Gould, W. (1984) *Japan's Reshaping of American Labour Law*, MIT Press, Mass.

Greenberg, J. (2001) *The Radical Face of the Ancient Constitution*, Cambridge University Press, Cambridge.

Grey, T.C. (1980) 'The Disintegration of Property', *Nomos*, XX11, New York University Press, New York.

Gutman, A (2001) 'Introduction', in M. Ignatieff (ed.), *Human Rights as Politics and Idolatory*, Princeton University Press, Princeton.

Gutman, A. and Ziegler, B. (1964) *Communism and the Courts*, D.C. Heath, Lexington.

Hackett, R. (1968) 'Political Modernisation and the Meiji Genro', in R.E. Ward (ed.), *Political Development in Modern Japan*, Princeton University Press, Princeton.

Haley, J.O. (1978) 'The Myth of the Reluctant Litigant', *Journal of Japanese Studies*, 8(2): 359.

Haley, J.O. (1982a) 'Sheathing the Sword of Justice in Japan: An Essay on Law without Sanctions', *Journal of Japanese Studies*, 8(2): 265.

Lukacs, G. (1922) *History and Class Consciousness*, reprinted by Merlin Press, London, 1968.

Lukes, S. and Skull, A. (eds) (1983) *Durkheim and the Law*, Martin Robertson, Oxford.

McCray-Pearson, J. (1993) 'The Federal and State Bills of Rights: An Historical Look', *Howard Law Journal*, 36(1): 43.

McGoldrick, D. (1991) *The Human Rights Committee*, Oxford University Press, Oxford.

MacIntyre, A. (1967) *A Short History of Ethics*, Routledge, London.

McLaren, W.W. (1965) *A Political History of Japan During the Meiji Era*, Frank Cass, London.

MacNeil, I.R. (1980) *The New Social Contract*, Yale University Press, New Haven.

Maitland, W.H. (1936) *The Forms of Action at Common Law*, Cambridge University Press, Cambridge.

Maki, J. (1962) *Government and Politics in Japan: The Road to Democracy*, Thames and Hudson, London.

Maki, J. (ed.) (1964) *Court and Constitution in Japan*, University of Washington Press, Seattle.

Maki, J. (trans and ed.) (1980) *Japan's Commission on the Constitution: The Final Report*, University of Washington Press, Seattle.

Mann, M. (1993) *The Sources of Social Power, vol. 2: The Rise of Classses and Nation-states, 1760–1914*, Cambridge University Press, Cambridge.

Marks, S. (2000) *The Riddle of All Constitutions*, Oxford University Press, Oxford.

Marshall, B. (1967) *Capitalism and Nationalism in Prewar Japan*, Stanford University Press, Stanford.

Marshall, T.H. (1949) 'Citizenship and Social Class', in B. Turner and P. Hamilton (eds) (reprinted 1994), *Citizenship: Critical Concepts*, Routledge: London.

Marsland, S.E. (1989) *The Birth of the Japanese Labour Movement*, University of Hawaii Press, Honolulu.

Marx, K. (1871) *Capital*, reprinted by Lawrence and Wishart, London, 1965.

Mason, A.T. (1958) *The Supreme Court from Taft to Warren*, Norton, New York.

Mason, A.T. and Beaney, W.M. (1959) *The Supreme Court in a Free Society*, Prentice-Hall, Englewood Cliffs.

Mauss, M. (1924) *The Gift: The Form and Reason for Exchange in Archaic Societies*, reprinted 1990, Routledge, London.

Mecham, P. (1936) 'The Jurisprudence of Despair', *Iowa Law Review*, 21(4): 672.

Mehren, A.T. van (ed.) (1963) *Law in Japan*, Harvard University Press, Cambridge, Mass.

Haley, J.O. (1982b) 'The Politics of Informal Justice: The Japanese Experience', in R.L. Abel (ed.) *The Politics of Informal Justice*, Academic Press, New York.

Haley, J. O. (1986) 'Japanese Administrative Law: Introduction,' *Law in Japan*, 19: 1.

Hall, J.W. (1968) 'A Modern Monarch for Modern Japan', in R.F. Ward (ed.), *Political Development in Modern Japan*, Princeton University Press, Princeton.

Hall, J.W. (1968) *Studies in the Institutional History of Early Modern Japan*, Princeton University Press, Princeton.

Hamano, S.B. (1999) 'Incomplete Revolutions and not so Alien Transplants: the Japanese Constitution and Human Rights', *University of Pennsylvania Journal of Constitutional Law*, 1(3): 415.

Hamelink, C. (1994) *The Politics of World Communication: A Human Rights Perspective*, Sage, London.

Hargreaves, R. (2002) *The First Freedom: A History of Free Speech*, Sutton Publishing, Stroud.

Hartz, L. (1968) *Economic Policy and Democratic Thought*, Quadrangle, Chicago.

Hay, D., Thompson, E. and Linebaugh, P. (1975) *Albion's Fatal Tree*, Allen Lane, London.

Held, D. (1997) *Models of Democracy*, Polity, Cambridge.

Held, D. (2004) *Global Covenant: The Social Democratic Alternative to the Washington Consensus*, Polity Press, Cambridge.

Henderson, D.F. (ed.) (1968a) *The Constitution of Japan: Its First Twenty Years*, University of Washington Press, Seattle.

Henderson, D.F. (1968b) 'Law and Political Modernisation in Japan', in R.E. Ward (ed.), *Political Development in Modern Japan*, Princeton University Press, Princeton.

Henderson, D.F. (1974) '"Contracts" in Tokugawa Japan', *The Journal of Japanese Studies*, 1(1): 51.

Henderson, D.F. (1977) *Conciliation and Japanese Law*, 2 vols, University of Washington Press, Seattle.

Henderson, D.F. (1980) 'Japanese Law in English: Reflections on Translation', *Journal of Japanese Studies*, 6(1): 117.

Henderson, D.F. and Haley, J. (eds) (1978) *Law and Legal Process in Japan*, University of Washington, mimeo.

Hill, C. (1971) *World Turned Upside Down*, Penguin, Harmondsworth.

Hindess, B. (1996) *Discourses of Power: From Hobbes to Foucault*, Blackwell, Oxford.

Hindess, B. and Hirst, P. (1977) *Pre-Capitalist Modes of Production*, Routledge, London.

Hingwan, K. (1996) 'Identity, Otherness and Human Rights in Japan', in

R. Goodman and I. Neary (eds) *Case Studies in Human Rights in Japan*, Curzon Books, Richmond.

Hirst, P. (1979) *Law and Ideology*, Macmillan, London.

Hohfeld, W. (1919) *Fundamental Legal Conceptions as Applied to Judicial Reasoning, and Other Legal Essays*, Yale University Press, New Haven.

Hooker, M.B. (1978) *A Concise Legal History of South-East Asia*, Oxford University Press, Oxford.

Horwitz, M. (1977) *The Transformation of American Law: 1780–1860*, Harvard University Press, Cambridge, Mass.

Horwitz, M. (1992) *The Transformation of American Law: 1870–1960: The Crisis of Legal Orthodoxy*, Oxford University Press, Oxford.

Howe, M. (1957, 1963) *Justice Oliver Wendell Holmes*, 2 vols, Belknap, Cambridge, Mass.

Hozumi, N. (1938) *Ancestor Worship and Japanese Law*, Hokuseido Press, Tokyo.

Hubert, H. and Mauss, M. (1979) *Sacrifice: Its Nature and Function*, Chicago University Press, Chicago.

Hunt, A. (1978) *The Sociological Movement in Law*, Macmillan, London.

Hunt, P. (1996) *Reclaiming Social Rights*, Ashgate-Dartmouth, Aldershot.

Hurst, J.W. (1950) *The Growth of American Law*, Little Brown, Boston.

Hurst, J.W. (1956) *Law and the Conditions of Freedom in the 19th Century United States*, University of Wisconsin Press, Madison.

Hurst, J.W. (1977) *Law and Social Order in the United States*, Cornell University Press, Ithaca.

Hurst, J.W. (1982) *Law and Markets in United States History*, University of Wisconsin Press, Madison.

Hurst, J.W. (1979) 'Old and New Dimensions of Research in US Legal History', *The American Journal of Legal History*, XXIII, p. 1.

Ignatieff, M. (2001) *Human Rights as Politics and Idolatory*, Princeton University Press, Princeton.

Irons, P.H. (2002) *Jim Crow's Children: The Broken Promise of the Brown Decision*, Viking, New York.

Ishay, M. (1997) *The Human Rights Reader*, Routledge, New York.

Ishii, R. (ed.) (1968) *Japanese Legislation in the Meiji Era*, Kasai, Tokyo.

Ishii, R. (1980) *A History of Political Institutions in Japan*, University of Tokyo Press, Tokyo.

Ishimine, K. (1974) *A Comparative Study of Judicial Review under American and Japanese Constitutional Law*, University Microfilms, Ann Arbor.

Ito, H. (1889) *Commentaries of the Constitution of the Empire of Japan*, Igirisu-Horitsu Gakko, Tokyo.

Itoh, H. (1970) 'How Judges Think in Japan', *The American Journal of Comparative Law*, 18: 775.

Itoh, H. and Beer, L. (eds) (1978) *The Constitutional Case Law of Japan:*

Selected Supreme Court Decisions, 1961–70, University of Washington Press, Seattle.

Jacobs, C. (1954) *Law Writers and the Courts*, University of California Press, Berkeley.

Jones, P. (1994) *Rights*, Macmillan, Basingstoke.

Jordan, W. (1974) *White over Black: American Attitudes to the Negro, 1550–1812*, North Carolina University Press, North Carolina.

Kairys, D. (ed.) (1982) *The Politics of Law*, Pantheon, New York.

Kant, I. (1797) 'Metaphysics of Morals', reprinted in M. Ishay (ed.) (1997) *The Human Rights Reader*, Routledge, New York.

Kennedy, D. (1976) 'Form and Substance in Private Law Adjudication', *Harvard Law Review*, 89(1): 1685.

Keyssar, A. (2000) *The Right to Vote: The Contested History of Democracy in the United States*, Basic Books, New York.

Kim, P. (1998) 'Darkness in the Land of the Rising Sun: How the Japanese Discriminate Against Ethnic Koreans Living in Japan', *Cardozo Journal of International and Comparative Law*, 4(2): 479.

Klug, F. (2000) *Values for a Godless Age*, Penguin, Harmondsworth.

Krieken, R. van (1989) 'Violence, Self-discipline and Modernity: Beyond the "Civilizing Process"', *Sociological Review*, 37(2): 193.

Krotoszynski, R. (1998) 'The Chrysanthemum, the Sword, and the First Amendment: Disentangling Culture, Community, and Freedom of Expression', *Wisconsin Law Review*, (4): 905.

Kuhn, T. (1970) *The Structure of Scientific Revolution*, University of Chicago Press, Chicago.

Langbein, J. (2003) *The Origins of Adversary Criminal Trial*, Oxford University Press, Oxford.

Langlois, A. (2001) *The Politics of Justice and Human Rights: Southeast Asia and Universalist Theory*, Cambridge University Press, Cambridge.

Lauren, P. (1998) *The Evolution of International Human Rights: Visions Seen*, University of Pennsylvania Press, Philadephia.

Lepard, B. (2002) *Rethinking Humanitarian Intervention*, Penn State Press, University Park, Philadelphia.

Lijnzaad, P. (1995) *Reservations to United Nations Human Rights Treaties* Martinus Nihof, Dordrecht.

Likosky, M. (ed.) (2002) *Transnational Legal Processes*, Butterworth London.

Locke, G. (1922) *History and Class Consciousness*, reprinted by Merlin Pre London, 1968.

Lopez, J. (2003) *Society and its Metaphors*, Continuum, London.

Lowi, T. (1969) *The End of Liberalism*, Norton, New York.

Luard, E. (1982) (1989) *A History of the United Nations*, 2 vols, Macmi Basingstoke.

Meillon, C. and Bunch, C. (2001) *Holding on to the Promise: Women's Human Rights and the Beijing+5 Review*, Center for Women's Global Leadership, Rutgers University, New Brunswick.

Melamed, D. and Westin, D. (1981) 'Anti-Intellectual History', *Yale Law Journal*, 90(4): 1497.

Merrils, J. (1988) *The Development of International Law by the European Court of Human Rights*, Manchester University Press, Manchester.

Mill, John Stuart (1859) *On Liberty*, reprinted by Oxford University Press, Oxford, 2000.

Miller, A.S. (1968) *The Supreme Court and American Capitalism*, Free Press, New York.

Miller, D. (1976) *Social Justice*, Oxford University Press, Oxford.

Miller, F.O. (1965) *Minobe Tatsukuchl: Interpreter of Constitutionalism in Japan*, University of California Press, Berkeley.

Mills, K. (1998) *Human Rights in the Emerging Global Order*, Macmillan, Basingstoke.

Milner, W. (2002) 'Economic Globalization and Rights: An Empirical Analysis', in A. Brysk (ed.), *Globalization and Human Rights*, University of California Press, Berkeley.

Milsom, S. (1981) *Historical Foundations of the Common Law*, Butterworth, London.

Minear, R. (1970) *Japanese Tradition and Western Law*, Harvard University Press, Cambridge, Mass.

Mitchell, R.H. (1976) *Thought Control in Prewar Japan*, Cornell University Press, Ithaca.

Moore, B. (1966) *Social Origins of Dictatorship and Democracy*, Penguin, Harmondsworth.

Moore, B. (1972) *Reflections on the Causes of Human Misery*, Allen Lane, London.

Moore, B. (1978) *Injustice: The Social Basis of Obedience and Revolt*, Macmillan, Basingstoke.

Morsink, J. (1999) *The Universal Declaration of Human Rights: Origins, Drafting and Intent*, University of Pennsylvania Press, Philadephia.

Mukai, K. and Toshitani, N. (1967) 'The Progress and Problems of Compiling the Civil Code in the Early Meiji Era', *Law in Japan*, 1: 1.

Murphy, C. (1994) *International Organization and Industrial Change*, Polity, Oxford.

Murphy, W. (1962) *Congress and the Courts*, University of Chicago Press, Chicago.

Muzaffar, Chandra (1993) *Human Rights and the New World Order*, Just World Trust, Penang.

Najita, T. (1974) *The Intellectual Origins of Modern Japanese Politics*, University of Chicago Press, Chicago.

Nakamura, H. (1960) *The Ways of Thinking of Eastern Peoples*, Unesco, Tokyo.

Nakamura, K. (1962) *The Formation of Modern Japan: As Viewed from Legal History*, The Centre for East Asian Cultural Studies, Tokyo.

Nakane, C. (1970) *Japanese Society*, Penguin, Harmondsworth.

Nakano, T. (1923) *The Ordinance Power of the Japanese Emperor*, Johns Hopkins University Press, Baltimore.

Neary, I. (2002) *Human Rights in Japan, South Korea and Taiwan*, Routledge, London.

Nelson, W. (1982) *The Roots of American Bureacracy, 1830–1900*, Harvard Univerity Press, Cambridge.

Noda, Y. (1976) *Introduction to Japanese Law*, University of Tokyo Press, Tokyo.

Novak, W. (1993) *The People's Welfare: Law and Regulation in Nineteenth-Century America*, University of North Carolina Press, Chapel Hill.

Nozick, R. (1974) *Anarchy, State and Utopia*, Basic Books, New York.

Nussbaum, M. (ed.) (2002) *For Love of Country*, Beacon Books, New York.

O'Byrne, D. (2003) *Human Rights: An Introduction*, Prentice-Hall, Harlow.

Oda, H. (2000) *Japanese Law*, Oxford University Press, Oxford.

Oppler, A.C. (1976) *Legal Reform in Occupied Japan: a Participant Looks Back*, Princeton University Press, Princeton, New Jersey.

Panitch, L. and Leys, C. (eds)(2003) *The New Imperial Challenge*, Merlin, London.

Pashukanis, E.B. (1978) *Law and Marxism*, Ink Links, London.

Pashukanis, E.B. (1980) *Selected Writings on Marxism and Law*, Academic Press, London and New York.

Paul, A. (1960) *Conservative Crisis and the Rule of Law – 1881–1895*, Cornell University Press, New York.

Paul, A.J. (1978) 'Legal progressivism, the Courts and the Crisis of the 1890s', in L.M. Friedman and H.N. Scheiber (eds), *American Law and the Constitutional Order*, Harvard University Press, Cambridge, Mass.

Pereira, W. (1997) *InHuman Rights: The Western System and Global Human Rights Abuse*, The Other India Press, Mapusa.

Pfeffer, L. (1965) *This Honourable Court*, Beacon, Boston.

Phillips, K. (1990) *The Politics of Rich and Poor*, Random House, New York.

Pittau, J. (1967) *Political Thought in Early Japan, 1868–1889*, Harvard University Press, Cambridge.

Pocock, J. (1974) *The Ancient Constitution*, Cambridge University Press, Cambridge.

Posner, R. (1981) *The Economics of Justice*, Harvard University Press, Cambridge, Mass.

Poulantzas, N. (1974) *Fascism and Dictatorship*, New Left Books, London.

Pound, R. (1909) 'Liberty of Contract', *Yale Law Journal*, 18: 454.

Primus, R. (1999) *The American Language of Rights*, Cambridge University Press, Cambridge.

Purcell, E.A. (1973) *The Crisis of Democratic Theory*, University Press of Kentucky, Lexington.

Poulantzas, N. (1974) *Fascism and Dictatorship*, New Left Books, London.

Quigley, H. and Turner, J. (1956) *The New Japan*, University of Minnesota Press, Minneapolis.

Qureshi, A. (1999) *International Economic Law*, Sweet and Maxwell, London.

Rajagopal, B. (2003) *International Law from Below*, Cambridge University Press, Cambridge.

Ramlogan, R. (1994) 'The Human Rights Revolution in Japan: A Story of New Wine in Old Wine Skins,' *Emory International Law Review*, 8(1): 127.

Rancharan, B.G. (1997) *The Principle of Legality in International Human Rights Institutions*, Martinus Nijhoff, The Hague.

Rawls, J. (1971) *A Theory of Justice*, Clarendon Press, Oxford.

Rawls, J. (1999) *The Law of Peoples*, Harvard University Press, Cambridge, Mass.

Reber, S-L. (1999) 'Buraku Mondai in Japan', *Harvard Journal of Human Rights*, 12(1): 297.

Renner, K. (1949) *The Institutions of the Private Law and their Social Functions*, Routledge, London.

Restatement of the Law of Contracts (1932) *American Law Institute*, St. Paul, Minn.

Rodenhamer, D. (1992) *Fair Trial: The Rights of the Accused in American History*, Oxford University Press, New York.

Rose, N. (1999) *Powers of Freedom*, Cambridge University Press, Cambridge.

Rueschemeyer, D., Stephens, E. and Stephens, J. (1992) *Capitalist Development and Democracy*, Polity Press, Cambridge.

Santos, B. de Sousa (1995) *Toward a New Common-Sense: Law, Politics and Science in a Paradigmatic Transition*, Routledge, New York.

Schieber, H. (1975) 'Federalism and the American Economic Order 1789–1920', *Law and Society Review*, 57: 59.

Schneiderman, D. (2000) 'Investment Rules and the New Constitutionalism', *Law and Social Inquiry*, 25(3): 757.

Schuler, M. (ed.)(1995) *From Basic Needs to Basic Rights: Women's Claim to Human Rights*, University of Pennsylvania Press, Philadelphia.

Schwartz, B. (1974) *The Law in America*, McGraw-Hill, New York.

Schwartz, B. (1977) *The Great Rights of Mankind: A History of the American Bill of Rights*, Oxford University Press, New York.

Schwartz, J. (1997) *The Illusion of Opportunity*, Norton, New York.

Seizelet, E. (1992) 'European Law and Tradition in Japan during the Meiji Era, 1868–1912', in Mommsen and de Moor (eds), *European*

Expansion and Law: The Encounter of European and Indigenous Law in Ninneteenmth- and Twentieth-Century Africa and Asia, Berg, Oxford.

Sellars, K. (2002) *The Rise and Rise of Human Rights*, Sutton Publishing, Stroud.

Sen, A. (1999a) *Development as Freedom*, Oxford University Press, Oxford.

Sen, A. (1999b) 'Human Rights and Economic Achievements', in J. Bauer and D. Bell (eds), *The East Asian Challenge for Human Rights*, Cambridge University Press, Cambridge.

Shapiro, M. (1964) *Law and Politics in the Supreme Court*, Free Press, Glencoe.

Shue, H. (1980) *Basic Rights: Subsistence, Affluence, and U.S. Foreign Policy*, Princeton University Press, Princeton.

Simpson, A.W. B. (1979) 'The Horwitz Thesis and the History of Contracts', *University of Chicago Law Review*, 46: 533.

Smart, C. (1989) *Feminism and the Power of the Law*, Routledge, London.

Smith, D. (1983) *Barrington Moore: Violence, Morality and Political Change*, Macmillan, Basingstoke.

Smith, J. and Barnes, T. (1975) *The English Legal System: Carryover to the Colonies*, W.A. Clark Memorial Library, Los Angeles.

Sohn, L. (1995) *Rights in Conflict: The United Nations and South Africa*, Transnational, New York.

Starr, J.B. (ed.) *The United States Constitution: Its birth, growth and Influence in Asia*, Hong Kong University, Hong Kong.

Steiner, H. and Alston, P. (eds)(1996), *International Human Rights in Context: Law, Politics, Morals*, Oxford University Press, Oxford.

Stephens, J. (1979) *The Transition from Capitalism to Socialism*, Macmillan, London.

Stevens, C.R., and Takahashi, K. (eds)(no date) *Materials on Japanese Law*, mimeo, Columbia University Law School.

Stevens, C.R. (1971) 'Modern Japanese Law as an Instrument of Comparison', *The American Journal of Comparative Law*, 19: 665.

Stevens, R. (1983) *Law School: Legal Education in the United States From the 1850s to the 1980s*, University of North Carolina Press, Chapel Hill.

Sugarman, D. (1983) 'Law, Economy and the State in England, 1750–1914: Some Major Issues', in D. Sugarman (ed.), *Legality, Ideology and the State*, Academic Press, London.

Sugarman, D. (1986) 'Legal Theory, the Common Law Mind and the Making of the Textbook Tradition', in W. Twining (ed.), *Karl Llewellyn and the Realist Movement*, Weidennfeld and Nicholson, London.

Sugeno, K. (1992) *Japanese Labor Law*, University of Washington Press, Seattle.

Summers, C.W. (1969) 'Collective Agreements and the Law of Contracts', *Yale Law Journal*, 78(2): 525.

Sutherland, A. (1967) *The Law at Harvard*, Harvard University Press, Cambridge, Massachusetts.

Takayanagi, K. (1976) 'A Century of Innovation: The Development of Japanese Law, 1868–1961', in H. Tanaka (ed.), *The Japanese Legal System*, University of Tokyo Press, Tokyo.

Tang, J. (ed.) (1995) *Human Rights and International Relations in the Asia-Pacific Region*, Pinter London.

Thornberry, P. (2002) *Indigenous Peoples and Human Rights*, Juris Publishers, New York.

Titmuss, R. (1959) *The Gift Relationship: From Human Blood to Social Policy*, Allen and Unwin, London.

Titmuss, R. (1987) *The Philosophy of Welfare*, Allen and Unwin, London.

Tolley, H. (1987) *The United Nations Commission on Human Rights*, Westview Press, Boulder.

Toshitani, N. (1976) 'Japan's Modern Legal System: Its Formation and Structure', *Annals of the Institute of Social Science*, 17.

Trombadori, D. (1991) *Michel Foucault: Remarks on Marx*, Semiotexte, New York.

Trust Fund for Human Security, The (2002) *What is Human Security?*, The Ministry of Foreign Affairs of Japan, Tokyo.

Turner, B.S. (1993) 'Outline of a Theory of Human Rights', *Sociology*, 27(3): 489.

Turner, B.S. (2002) 'Cosmopolitan Virtue, Globalization and Patriotism', in *Theory, Culture and Society*, 19(1–2): 45.

Turner, B. and Hamilton, P. (eds) (1994) *Citizenship: Critical Concepts*, Routledge, London.

Tushnet, M. (1983) 'Following the Rules Laid Down', *Harvard Law Review*, 96(1): 4.

Twine, F. (1994) *Citizenship and Social Rights*, Sage, London.

Twining, W. (1973) *Karl Llewellyn and the Realist Movement*, Weidenfield and Nicholson, London.

Twiss, B. (1962) *Lawyers and the Constitution*, Russel and Russel, New York.

Ukai, N.W., Nathanson, N. (1968) 'Protection of Property Rights and Due Process of Law in the Japanese Constitution', in D.F. Henderson (ed.), *The Constitution of Japan: Its First Twenty Years*, University of Washington Press, Seattle.

Umegaki, M. (1988) *After the Restoration: The Beginnings of Japan's Modern State*, New York University Press, New York.

Upham, F. (1987) *Law and Social Change In Postwar Japan*, Harvard University Press, Cambridge Mass.

Uyehara, G. (1910) *The Political Development of Japan*, Constable, London.

Vaneigem, Raoul (2003) *A Declaration of the Rights of Human Beings*, Pluto, London.

Vincent, J. (1986) *Human Rights and International Relations*, Cambridge University Press, Cambridge.

Ward, R.E. (1957) 'The Origins of the Present Japanese Constitution', in H. Tanaka (ed.) (1976) *The Japanese Legal System*, University of Tokyo Press, Tokyo.

Ward, R.E. (ed.)(1968) *Political Development in Modern Japan*, Princeton University Press, Princeton.

Weber, M. (1978) *Economy and Society*, 2 vols, University of California, Berkeley.

Weber, M. (1980) *The General Economic History*, Transaction Books, New York.

White, G.E. (1976) *The American Judicial Tradition*, Oxford University Press, London and New York.

White, G.E. (1980) *Tort Law in America: An Intellectual History*, Oxford University Press, New York.

Winston, M. (ed.)(1989) *The Philosophy of Human Rights*, Wadsworth Publishing Company, Belmont.

Woodiwiss, A. (1990a) *Social Theory After Postmodernism: Rethinking Production, Law and Class*, Pluto, London.

Woodiwiss, A. (1990b) *Rights v. Conspiracy: A Sociological Essay on the Development of Labour Law in the United States*, Berg, Oxford.

Woodiwiss, A. (1992) *Law, Labour and Society in Japan: From Repression to Reluctant Recognition*, Routledge, London.

Woodiwiss, A. (1993) *Postmodernity USA: The Crisis of Social Modernism in Postwar America*, Sage, London.

Woodiwiss, A. (1998) *Globalisation, Human Rights and Labour Law in Pacific Asia*, Cambridge University Press, Cambridge.

Woodiwiss, A. (2001) *The Visual in Social Theory*, Athlone, London.

Woodiwiss, A. (2002) 'Human rights and the challenge of cosmopolitanism', *Theory, Culture and Society*, 19(1–2): 139.

Woodiwiss, A. (2003) *Making Human Rights Work Globally*, Glasshouse, London.

INDEX